IF YOU DO THIS⌐

Your Church
May Not
Recognize Their
New Youth Pastor

IF YOU DO THIS

Your Church
May Not
Recognize Their
New Youth Pastor

POWER 2 GROW
M I N I S T R I E S

JONES

TROY

Published by Power2Grow Publishing, Renton, WA 98057.

ISBN 0-9708366-0-0=0A

One night before bedtime, Chelsey, my seven-year-old daughter, said with excitement, "Daddy, I have a title for your new book."

I said, "Chelsey, what would you like Daddy to call his book?"

She thought a minute. "This is your second book?"

"Yes."

While bouncing on her bed, she said, "I think you should call it *Troy's Story Two.*"

I dedicate this book to the pride of my life: Kaylee and Chelsey Jones. Besides your mommy, you are the greatest gifts God has ever given to me. I am proud of you both. Having the two of you in my life is what *Troy's Story Two* is all about.

Acknowledgments

There are so many people who have made this book possible.

Thank you . . .

- Jana Jones, my wife. I couldn't have written this book without your encouragement. Your love and support is what gives me the strength to write.
- Michelle DeMonnin, project manager. Your creativity and commitment to excellence is why this book is what it is today.
- Stacy Newell. Thank you for editing and reading this book countless times. No one will ever understand how your ideas, suggestions, and input impacted this book.
- Rick Ross, my pastor. God has used you to be my mentor, pastor, and friend. Thanks for believing in me.
- Loran Lichty. Thank you for encouraging me to write. You have taught me so many principles in this book. In many ways you should be credited as the coauthor.

- Vic Lipsey. For your continuous excellence in editing and your insightful recommendations.
- Nik Baumgart. For typesetting this book and your personal encouragement.
- Doreen Dolleman, Aimee Lenger, Larry Lichty, and Randy McMillan. For taking your time to read the final manuscript and fine-tuning over and over again.

Foreword

I can't think of a better book for any youth pastor to read than this one. It will change your attitude and the way you do ministry. That's because the principles Troy writes about come directly from his own life; they are not just theories he read somewhere. He combines conviction and practicality like very few leaders can.

Troy uses the interaction between Jethro and Moses as the thesis of this book because Troy chases after leaders like Jethro to help him grow. As one of those leaders who have been instrumental in Troy's life, I can tell you that Troy practices what he preaches. He is the most teachable young man I have ever worked with. So when he writes about being teachable, he is again writing from his own life.

When Troy gives insights about building a team, I encourage you to listen, because I've seen no one better than he is at team building. When he writes about attitude, you are seeing right into his heart.

As their senior pastor, I have seen Troy and Jana grow in the last thirteen years. I promise you that Troy writes directly from a life of experience and success. This book challenges me personally. I encourage every youth pastor, leader, and senior pastor to read this book.

DR. RICK ROSS
SENIOR PASTOR, RENTON ASSEMBLY
RENTON, WASHINGTON

Contents

Chapter 1

The Day Moses Became a Leader

S tudents don't need a new program; they need a new leader.

The greatest need for youth ministry in America is for youth pastors and aspiring ministers to discover the leader within them. The principles in this book will change the way you do youth ministry by helping you become the right leader. *Leading* will make your youth ministry explode. Your church may not even recognize their "new" youth pastor if you apply the principles in this book. The day you become a leader is the day your youth ministry will change. However, if you stagnate, your youth ministry will stagnate.

Stop looking for the latest idea or new program to build your youth ministry. Stop blaming the curriculum. That's not the problem; you're the problem. If programs could build a great youth ministry, there would be a great youth ministry in every community of America. The only way to build a great youth ministry is to build a great you.

There has never been a greater day for youth ministry in the church. We have a window of opportunity to reach a new generation known as the *Millennials*. The Millennials represent 7.2 million young people born after 1982, comprising 28 percent of our population. They are the second largest generation in existence, after their parents, the Baby Boomers. The Millennials may even surpass the Baby Boomers in population.*

> ## To be effective in youth ministry, you must grow as a leader.

They will shape the morals and values of the twenty-first century.

The Millennials do not think creativity consists of an icebreaker or a quick gimmick out of some old *101 Ideas Youth Ministry Manual* written over a decade ago. These students spend their days conducting research instantly on the Internet. They will not stomach a leader who isn't prepared. To be effective in youth ministry, you must grow as a leader. If you don't change and grow, you will be obsolete in five years. Think about the reality of that statement: If you grow and learn new skills, your greatest day for youth ministry is looking you straight in the face. The decision is yours: Grow or become obsolete.

Goodbye to the "Kid" Youth Pastor

The role of the youth pastor is changing in the twenty-first century. The first concept of youth ministry took place in the forties when the "youth culture" was born. In the 1940s, the concept of youth ministry consisted of entertainment. Young people often had nothing to do on a Saturday night, so the church met the need with banana-split parties, fundraisers, activity groups, and social gatherings. While this entertainment approach was effective then, it doesn't work in the twenty-first century.

We live in a day that brings new opportunities, new challenges, and new problems. The rise of the Millennial generation must cause us to rethink the way we do youth ministry. Every church and youth leader must face the reality that the Millennials are different. They are optimistic, educated, and comfortable with technology. They are the

---

* Vicki Joyal, "Meet the Millennials", *News Now* (April 23, 2000) p. 1.

first high-tech generation born into a world of computers, cell phones, ATMs, and the Internet. If we are going to reach these teens, different values and approaches are required.

In the twenty-first century, youth pastors will be characterized with leadership, personal growth, team building, longevity, empowerment, and vision. Today's youth pastor must put aside the attitudes of being a kid and embrace the qualities of a leader. Stop asking, "How can I relate to the students?" and begin asking, "How can I lead students?" If you're a kid, you'll try to *relate* to students. That's wrong. You need to *lead* them. The following is a chart that illustrates the difference between a kid youth pastor and a leader.

YOUTH PASTORS

Kid	Leader
• Desires a mentor	• Chases after mentors
• Stagnates	• Grows daily
• Promotes programs	• Casts vision
• Makes excuses	• Takes responsibility
• Platitude attitude	• Winning attitude
• Repeats himself	• Reinvents himself
• Does everything	• Understands what must be done
• Involves students	• Involves everyone
• Builds programs	• Builds a team
• Hypes students up	• Empowers people
• Talks	• Listens
• Seeks advice	• Follows advice

The Day Moses Became a Leader

Exodus 18 describes how Moses successfully led the Israelites. By current standards he had the largest and most effective youth ministry in the nation. However, even Moses had trouble understanding when it was time to stop being the kid and grow as a leader.

Jethro, his father-in-law, was about to give Moses some of the most difficult instruction he had ever received. There is no doubt that Jethro was concerned about his daughter and her relationship with Moses. Moses had just sent his wife away because of his busy schedule. Moses must have thought, *What is my father-in-law doing here? What has my wife been saying about me?* Moses didn't understand that the next few days of his life would determine his destiny.

Moses had a "Jethro Experience" that taught him what ministry and leadership is all about. Every youth pastor needs a Jethro Experience. It causes you to change the way you think, the way you do ministry, and most importantly, the way you live.

Jethro told Moses it was time for him to become a leader and stop doing unproductive things. It was time for Moses to stop depending on yesterday's successes and learn new skills and principles for his ministry. It was time for him to lead. You have the chance today to put into practice the same principles that Jethro gave to Moses.

> **If you are not ready to change, put this book down and save yourself some time.**

The greatest weakness among youth pastors is that they minister to students without a team of empowered adults around them. They overwork themselves and then complain about it. The advice that Jethro gave to Moses will help you create a healthy environment to grow your youth ministry. Like students today, the Israelites needed a new leader, not a new idea.

If you do this and God so commands, you will be able to stand the strain, and all these people will go home satisfied. (Exodus 18:23)

Jethro said, "Moses, if you do this . . ." But all of the advice that Jethro gave him would have been meaningless if Moses hadn't put it into practice. It is very easy to read a book or attend a conference on youth ministry. It takes no intelligence to get excited about becoming a strong leader. But your church will not be impressed with your new information; they want to see a new you. Start by changing something you are doing today. Remember, "If you *do* this . . ." not if you *read* this, if you *believe* this, if you *preach* this, if you *feel* this, or if you *want* this. If you are not ready to change, put this book down and save yourself some time. However, if you apply these leadership principles, you will grow as a leader, have a healthy marriage, and will become a youth pastor who can effectively lead the Millennials.

The following story tells about the day Moses became a leader. It was the day Moses saved his family, ministry, the nation of Israel, and, most importantly, himself.

Exodus 18:5–27 (emphasis added)

Jethro, Moses' father-in-law, together with Moses' sons and wife, came to him in the desert, where he was camped near the mountain of God. Jethro had sent word to him, *"I, your father-in-law Jethro, am coming to you* with your wife and her two sons."

So Moses went out to meet his father-in-law and bowed down and kissed him. They greeted each other and then went into the tent. Moses told his father-in-law about everything the LORD had done to Pharaoh and the Egyptians for Israel's sake and about all the hardships they had met along the way and how the LORD had saved them.

Jethro was delighted to hear about all the good things the LORD had done for Israel in rescuing them from the hand of the Egyptians. He said, "Praise be to the LORD, who rescued you from the hand of the Egyptians and of Pharaoh, and who rescued the people from the hand of the Egyptians. Now I know that the LORD is greater than all other gods, for he did this to those who had treated Israel arrogantly." Then Jethro, Moses' father-in-law, brought a burnt offering and other sacrifices to God, and Aaron came with all the elders of Israel to eat bread with Moses' father-in-law in the presence of God.

The next day Moses took his seat to serve as judge for the people, and *they stood around him* from morning till evening. When his father-in-law saw all that Moses was doing for the people, he said, *"What is this you are doing* for the people? *Why do you alone sit as judge*, while all these people stand around you from morning till evening?"

Moses answered him, *"Because the people come to me* to seek God's will. Whenever they have a dispute, it is brought to me, and I decide between the parties and inform them of God's decrees and laws."

Moses' father-in-law replied, *"What you are doing is not good*. You and these people who come to you will only wear yourselves out. The work is too heavy for you; you cannot handle it alone. Listen now to me and I will give you some advice, and may God be with you. *You must* be the people's representative before God and bring their disputes to him. Teach them the decrees and laws, and show them the way to live and the duties they are to perform. *But select capable men* from all the people—men who fear God, trustworthy men who hate dishonest gain—and *appoint them as officials* over thousands, hundreds, fifties, and tens. *Have them serve* as judges for the people at all times, but have them bring every difficult case to you; the simple cases they can decide themselves. That will make your load lighter, because they will share it with you. *If you do this* and God so commands, you will be able to stand the strain, and all these people will go home satisfied."

Moses listened to his father-in-law and did everything he said. He chose capable men from all Israel and made them leaders of the people, officials over thousands, hundreds, fifties, and tens. They served as judges for the people at all times. The difficult cases they brought to Moses, but the simple ones they decided themselves.

Then Moses sent his father-in-law on his way, and Jethro returned to his own country.

Chapter 2

I Am Coming
to You

Jethro had sent word to him, "I, your father-in-law, am coming to you
with your wife and her two sons." So Moses went out to meet his
father-in-law and bowed down and kissed him. (Exodus 18:6–7)

L
eaders chase after mentors.

Moses was so caught up in his ministry that he didn't see the
issues hindering his personal growth and ministry. Success blinded
him. God sent Jethro to give Moses a wake-up call. Moses' ministry
was not the only thing at stake. His marriage, spiritual growth, and the
nation of Israel were also in jeopardy.

Great leaders chase after mentors; they don't wait for mentors to
chase after them. Moses should have been proactive about his personal growth and started looking. Stop desiring a mentor in your life
and begin chasing one. Every youth pastor needs a personal coach.
Coaches bring out the best in their players. They aren't interested in
making you a clone. They examine your individual gifts and talents
and direct you to be the best possible you. You don't have to like

them; they just need to know the game better than you. A good coach will motivate you to work and grow, not drink coffee and chat about your feelings.

Stop expecting leaders to mentor you on your own terms. Your view and definition of a mentor could be the very obstacle that prevents someone from personally mentoring you.

- A *leader* defines a mentor as, "Anyone who will help me grow."
- A *kid* defines a mentor as, "Someone who will invest an incredible amount of time in me."

Broaden your definition of mentorship and embrace the people God has brought into your life to impact you.

> Jethro was delighted to hear about all the good things the Lord had done for Israel in rescuing them from the hand of the Egyptians. (Exodus 18:9)

Jethro encouraged Moses and then evaluated his ministry. After he learned what Moses was doing, he laid out a step-by-step personal growth plan. (Details in chapter 8.)

You may be saying, "If I had someone like Jethro to encourage me, I would listen." You are living in a fantasy world if you think every mentor is going to be like Jethro. If you need someone to encourage you before you can grow, you'll miss the greatest teaching in your life. Some of the best mentors may never say a word to you.

It is your responsibility to chase after mentors and learn leadership. Stop complaining! That shows a lack of initiative. If you don't have enough initiative in your life to find a mentor, you don't deserve a mentor. This may sound brutal, but you need a wake-up call to stop whining and begin taking practical steps to find someone who will invest in your life.

I Am Coming to You

God sends people to encourage us, correct us, and give us insight and direction. It's one thing to want a mentor; it's another to get one. Your success as a leader is determined by your response when you hear a mentor say, "I am coming to you."

The next time a leader says he or she is coming to you, you need to say:

1. "I have time"

> So Moses went out to meet his father-in-law and bowed down and kissed him. (Exodus 18:7)

I have great mentors and coaches in my life because I am willing to pay the price. I drop everything when a mentor announces, "I am coming to see you." To spend a few moments with Rick Ross, my senior pastor, I would mow his lawn, housesit for him, take him to the airport early in the morning—whatever it took. It is not the responsibility of your senior pastor to make time for you. It is your responsibility to make time for them and get on their schedule. Learn the best way to communicate and hang out with them.

> ### Some of the best mentors may never say a word to you.

2. "I am ready to listen"

> Moses told his father-in-law about everything the LORD had done to Pharaoh and the Egyptians for Israel's sake. . . . (Exodus 18:8)

Leaders who have something valuable to say will not say it unless you are listening. Moses knew that Jethro had some critical advice, so

Moses began defending himself, trying to impress his father-in-law while hiding behind his successes. In reality, Moses put pride before his ministry responsibilities. Moses should have just shut his mouth and listened to the person who had more insight. Fortunately, by the end of his Jethro Experience, Moses had stopped talking and started listening.

3. *"I am teachable"*

The greatest characteristic that a youth pastor can have is teachability. Stop complaining, "My senior pastor doesn't mentor me." It indicates that you don't understand the mentoring process. If you are teachable, anyone can mentor you. If you're not willing to be coached, why should anyone waste his or her time? Many youth pastors talk about being teachable but few actually are. It shows when their senior pastor talks to them about something personal—like a lack of professionalism.

> **A teachable person doesn't pick and choose what to be taught.**

- "I'm comfortable talking about my ministry, but don't talk to me about being on time to the office."
- "Let's talk about youth, but not how I treat my spouse."
- "I'd like ideas on how to preach better, but please don't bring up my finances."

A teachable person doesn't pick and choose what to be taught. I remember the day that my senior pastor talked to me about my weight—a sensitive subject, to say the least. I could have responded, "Why is this any of your business?" But, since then, he has helped me with how I dress, my spending habits, attitudes, and even areas in which my wife, Jana, needed to grow.

Are you truly humble? Do you have a servant's heart? Are you ready for a mentor to discuss the way you treat your spouse, spend your money, exercise, dress, or need to change your attitude? If not, you're not ready to learn how to be a great leader.

4. "I am ready to change"

Change is difficult. We can say, "I have time. . . . I am ready to listen. . . . I am teachable." But your character strengthens when you actually change. Great leaders don't have the time or patience to waste with people who won't change. Good coaches want to stretch you beyond belief—and see results.

Three Levels of Mentors

There are three types of mentors every youth pastor needs for positive growth.

Level 1: Influential Mentors

PURPOSE: Influence
RELATIONSHIP: No relationship needed
FORMAT: Speaking, writing, opportunities to watch their ministries
IMPACT: To improve ministry effectiveness

You may not meet an influential mentor personally, but his or her books, conferences, and tapes improve the way you conduct your ministry. Some of my influences are John Maxwell, Tommy Barnett, and Rick Warren. These men have helped to shape my spiritual and organizational thinking.

You need leaders in your life who influence you. If you can't name leaders who are influencing you, you won't find a mentor to take you to the next level.

Level 2: Instructional Mentors

PURPOSE: Instruction

RELATIONSHIP: Occasional relationship

FORMAT: Speaking, writing, teaching, observation

IMPACT: To improve ministry thinking

You need mentors in your life who make you think. Leaders look for people who will challenge their minds. They understand that the influence of others will improve ministry effectiveness. The mentors who instruct me are people like District Superintendent Warren Bullock, Dr. Don Argue, Dr. Mel Ming—and the list goes on. I occasionally sit down with these people just to ask advice.

Seek out mentors who will instruct you. It alarms me when I meet youth pastors who don't continue their education with reading or annual conferences. They won't be effective leaders or youth pastors.

Level 3: Investment Mentors

PURPOSE: Time investment

RELATIONSHIP: Continuous relationship

FORMAT: Speaking, writing, teaching, observation, one-on-one interaction

IMPACT: To improve ministry growth

This is the highest mentoring level. Your initiative is required. These relationships don't arrive in your life by accident. They take time and energy. I have mentors like this because I schedule time for them. Then I ask good questions, listen carefully, observe everything they do, and then ask more questions.

If you don't learn from influential and instructional mentors, you will never develop leaders who will personally invest in your life. The first step of mentoring doesn't begin with investment; it begins by learning from leaders with whom you currently have no personal relationship.

How Do I Find Mentors?

1. Become a lifelong learner

Lifelong learners never stop the learning process. They love to read books to improve their marriage, finances, leadership skills, spiritual disciplines, and their ministry. If you only study youth ministry, you will never be a great leader.

> **Never stop learning and you will keep leading.**

Lifelong learners invest money into growth. They always budget to continue their education, buy another book, attend a conference, or have lunch with a mentor.

Never stop learning and you will keep leading.

2. Identify leaders you want for mentors

Sit down and write a list of the mentors you want. Once you have identified them, read all of their books, listen to their tapes, and attend their churches and conferences. Do whatever it takes to be exposed to their motivations and ministry.

3. Learn from everybody

Leaders learn from everybody. If you don't have a mentor, you're not learning from the people who God has placed in your life already. Why would God bring another mentor your way when you can't learn from your spouse, senior pastor, or a close friend?

I have learned from kids, a waiter, by watching a movie, or just walking through a mall. I learn from men who are better husbands. I learn from those who have kids serving God. I learn from people who spend their money wisely. The greatest strength in my life is that I have trained myself to learn from everybody.

I Am Coming to You

4. Engage leaders in questions

Very few of my mentors sat down and decided to mentor me. I developed a relationship by habitually asking questions of them. Schedule a lunch with someone you want to influence you. While eating, don't just sit there and expect great words of wisdom to begin pouring from their lips. Get out your list of questions and begin asking.

Listen to what the leader doesn't say as well as what he does. Many times a great leader doesn't have an immediate response. Your job is to keep asking questions and listen.

Don't start by asking personal questions, and never ask questions that will put a leader in an awkward situation. You have to earn credibility first. Ask questions that are open and reflective in nature. For example, ask, "How can someone grow their relationship with his or her spouse? How does a person grow in prayer?" Don't ask, "How do you spend time with your spouse? What time do you pray every day?"

5. Watch leaders lead

A great leader doesn't have to spend an ounce of time with you to be a good mentor. When you are teachable, you will grow by watching. When I attend a conference or church service of one of my mentors, I watch what they do before and after the service. On vacation, I remember following Rick Warren around his church, just watching him hang around people. I learned so much from him by seeing how he connects with people, how he walks slowly, and how he carries himself.

6. Understand that mentors are not perfect

No mentor or coach is perfect. Although they should be consistent with their advice, sometimes they are not. Don't concentrate on their weaknesses, but focus on their strengths. Wisdom is required of a great leader. Wisdom means you recognize that no one is perfect and no one has all of the answers. Wisdom accepts the reality that you can learn from someone who is still on the journey of personal growth.

A True Jethro Experience

I have met many youth pastors who want a mentor but few who really know the cost. A true Jethro Experience may hurt, but it will change you for the better.

My passion is to develop and train young ministers. One of the great interns I had was Pat Hartsfield. Pat was raised and called into full-time ministry as a student in my youth ministry. I remember the day he became a leader. He kept saying to me,

Leaders learn from everybody.

"I want some time with you. Will you mentor me?" We set a time to get together at 8:00 A.M. on Saturday at a local restaurant.

I arrived early, excited about mentoring Pat. I sat in the restaurant and waited. Pat didn't show. Frustrated, I thought, *He is only talk. If Pat really wanted me to invest in him, he would be here.*

I decided to really invest in Pat's life that day and headed for his workplace. About 10:00 A.M. I showed up and announced, "I am coming to you." Pat was shocked. During his break, we sat down in the back room and I said, "Pat, are you ready for me to invest in your life?" The next few minutes became Pat's Jethro Experience.

"Pat, you don't really want a mentor. You have no respect for my time. One day you will be a youth pastor and forget an appointment with your senior pastor. He should fire you. Do you know what I had to do to be with you this morning? I could've been meeting with someone else. I could've awakened my girls today. I could've taken my wife out for breakfast. I could've been reading. But I wanted to be with you. I scheduled my day around you, and you forgot."

Pat is a great guy, but great guys don't necessarily get mentored. Pat needed to show initiative and chase after me, not me after him.

Today, Pat is a great youth pastor. If you talk to Pat, he will recall that Saturday morning as his Jethro Experience. He didn't just hear me that day; he changed. A light came on and Pat understood for the first time that mentorship is more than a desire. He understood that if he was going to have leaders invest in him, he needed to be responsible and show up to the meeting.

**12 Leadership Qualities of the
Twenty-First Century Youth Pastor**

Leaders chase 1 after mentors.

Chapter 3

They Stood Around Him

The next day Moses took his seat to serve as judge for the people, and they stood around him from morning till evening. (Exodus 18:13)

. . . all these people stand around you from morning till evening. (Exodus 18:14)

Leaders grow.
Jethro spent the day watching Moses minister to the people. Moses was in the office early, and didn't have a clue there was a problem. He just wanted to show off to Dad and maybe teach him a few things. Moses was so caught up in his own success that he didn't know his ministry was ineffective and the people were frustrated. People just stood around him all day.

What's the problem with this picture? If Moses spent all day ministering to people, when did he have time to grow personally? When did Moses pray? When did Moses have time for his family? When did he have time to build a team or learn new skills? Jethro understood that

Moses was more in love with the call of his ministry than God's plan for his ministry. Jethro knew that Moses had to change. So he gave Moses a step-by-step, personal growth plan that required changes in his daily routine. (Details in chapter 8.)

If you are too busy to grow, you are too busy. The kid youth pastor says, "I don't have time to . . ." Of course, there is never time to do the things God hasn't called you to do. The enemy wants you to be busy. Busy people stagnate. Busy people don't enjoy life; they don't take time to get stronger. The worst thing in the world is to be so busy that you don't have time to read a book. The only way to be effective in youth ministry is to keep growing. You either grow daily or die gradually.

> **You either grow daily or die gradually.**

The Cost of Growth

One reason youth pastors don't grow is that growth is hard work. But remember, you either grow now or pay a high price for missed opportunities later in life.

1. *Grow, so your family will grow*

> After Moses had sent away his wife Zipporah, his father-in-law Jethro received her. (Exodus 18:2)

Why did Jethro show up to Moses' ministry? Because Moses was too busy for his family; he sent away his wife and kids. You are called to minister to your family *before* students. If you can't take care of your bride, why would God let you take care of his?

A leader understands that a healthy family and youth ministry should coexist. This is not an either-or situation. You can't afford to compromise either one. There is nothing worse than a youth pastor blaming family for his or her own lack of responsibility.

Recently, I had a youth pastor cancel an appointment at the last minute because it conflicted with a commitment to his spouse. He said, "You know, family has to be first."

I said, "This has nothing to do with your family. You are missing this appointment because you need to grow as a leader. Stop blaming your wife that you don't plan ahead and write things down on a calendar.

> **If you can't take care of your bride, why would God let you take care of his?**

Take responsibility for your actions. You're making your spouse look bad when actually you are the one who is disorganized."

The only way I can encourage my wife and two little girls to grow is by growing myself. Some of your spouses are bitter because you are bitter. Some of them don't want to show up to youth services because you really don't want to be there either. People ask me all the time, "Troy, how do you bring out the best in your spouse? How do you encourage your spouse?" Simple: Keep growing. As I grow, Jana grows.

2. Grow, so your ministry will grow

Your ministry will only grow as big as you are. If your youth ministry is dying, you are dying. If your youth ministry is praying, you are praying. Are they full of energy? You are full of energy. Your students reflect you. If you don't grow, you won't be saved by a new idea, program, or brainstorming session.

3. Grow, so your compensation will grow

In the church, money can be an awkward subject. You get paid for what you do because that is what you are worth. I understand that we don't do ministry for the money. But do you know why God trusts me with money? I have proven myself to be trustworthy. Why would God give you a financial blessing when you waste what he is giving you now? Why would your senior pastor give you a raise when you are not worth what the church is paying you presently?

Simple leadership rule: Be worth more than what you're being paid. If you have a $10.00-an-hour job, work like you're receiving $20.00 an hour. If your church pays you $25,000, work like they pay you $40,000. Why? You'll keep the job longer, and eventually someone will pay you what you are worth.

4. Grow, so your leadership team will grow

The reason why some youth pastors only have a bunch of college students working with them is because of their own lack of personal growth. Stop complaining about the "losers" that you have working for you and come to grips with your leadership ability. Why would the CEO of a company work with you if you can't be on time to the office? Why would that busy mother give her time if she can organize towels better than you can organize a retreat? Your leadership team is a reflection of *you.*

5. Grow, so your students will grow

Programs don't grow students; leaders grow students. If you think you can put your students in a discipleship program so they will grow on their own, you are fooling yourself. If you want your students to memorize scriptures, you have to memorize scriptures. Do you want students to pray? Do it yourself. Do you want students to read their Bibles? Read your Bible. Your students will grow if *you* grow.

6. Grow, so you can lead others to change

Why is it that some leaders can lead effective change and others get crucified for suggesting it? People aren't necessarily resistant to change, but they do react to *how* and *who* leads it. The leader must have character and credibility. The only way to build a life of character and credibility is to keep growing.

Some may wonder, "How did the church allow you to turn the building into an activity center for a bunch of street kids? . . . How could you shoot off fireworks in a brand new building?" Well, I never stopped growing as a leader. My personal growth gave me the credibility and character to lead the church in effective change.

7. Grow, so you will stay in youth ministry

Longevity is crucial in youth ministry. There are many reasons why people leave their ministry, but one reason is that they stop growing as leaders. Then one day they wake up and realize that they are totally irrelevant and ineffective to their generation. You will not make it in youth ministry without a commitment to a personal growth plan.

**12 Leadership Qualities of the
Twenty-First Century Youth Pastor**

1 Leaders chase after mentors.

2 Leaders grow daily.

Chapter 4

What Is This You Are Doing?

When his father-in-law saw all that Moses was doing for the people, he said, "What is this you are doing for the people?" (Exodus 18:14)

L eaders have a clear vision.

After Jethro reviewed Moses' ministry, Moses expected his father-in-law to say, "I am proud of you, Son." Instead, Jethro looked Moses straight in the eyes and asked him the most important question for any leader, "What is this you are doing?" Leaders ask tough questions, the kind of questions that force you to think about your vision and direction in ministry.

Every once in a while you need to stop and ask yourself, "What am I doing?" A kid youth pastor will feel good when he is busy, because being busy is how he defines success. He does whatever makes him comfortable.

However, a leader will ask some basic questions on a regular basis:

- "What am I really doing for these students?"
- "Do I really understand the students I am trying to reach?"
- "Why would a Millennial want to attend my youth ministry?"

Why Vision?

Where there is no revelation, the people cast off restraint. (Proverbs 29:18)

Three things will be greatly hindered if you don't have a vision from God.

- Your youth ministry
- Your daily schedule
- Your leadership team

Leaders know where they are going and they have a clear vision of the future. It doesn't matter if you have a title, all the training in the world, or are involved with all the programs in your denomination; if you haven't heard from God and know where you are going, you are not the leader.

1. To build a healthy youth ministry

Without a vision you can't answer the question, "What am I really doing for these students?" A great leader can answer with confidence. He knows exactly what he should and shouldn't be doing. Jethro confronted Moses with these basic questions, "Moses, who are you trying to impress? What are you doing?"

Stop right now and think about why you are doing ministry. Who are you trying to impress by being busy? Do you have a compelling vision that will build a healthy youth ministry? Be honest with yourself: Do you really know your core values and vision as a leader? You will never build a healthy youth ministry if you don't know where you're going.

2. To be efficient

Moses was so busy he didn't have time to ask, "What am I doing?" Everyone stood around him from morning until evening. His ministry and daily duties were more important to him than the people. Even so, no one was impressed that Moses didn't spend time at home in the evenings or take a day off. Fortunately, Jethro made Moses stop and evaluate his life.

> **Vision gives you the clarity to say yes and no to commitments.**

Busyness will kill a youth pastor. Vision gives you the clarity to say yes and no to commitments. I have talked to many youth pastors about their schedules. They almost pride themselves in the fact that they are never home. You will never be a great leader if you don't have time to stop and reflect on what you are doing.

3. To attract great leaders

Leaders are motivated by vision. If you think small, you will never attract great leaders. The adults in your church will only give you their time if they know they are giving it to a vision that will make a difference. Take an honest look at your present youth leaders and team. The strength and quality of your team speaks loudly about your vision. Is your vision capable of attracting great leaders? Have you heard from God in such a way that people will want to follow you?

What You Need to Do to Get a Guy Like Me to Work with You

Every person wants significance and value. Everyone wants to be involved in a ministry that makes a difference.

One of the greatest leaders I have today is Loran Lichty, a businessman at my church who worked for Alaska Airlines. He's married with two kids and has the skills to go anywhere in life.

One Sunday evening I paraded the "changed lives" before the church. While the students gave their testimonies, Loran and his wife, Brenda, watched with tears rolling down their faces. After I shared my vision of changing a generation, Loran wrote me a check for $50.00. "Use this money to change more lives," he said. I never asked him. I never begged him. I just stood before the people and poured out my heart. He was so moved that he had to get involved.

> **You must have a vision that is worthy of their time.**

Loran became my right-hand man. We did some creative illustrated messages together. In fact, one message filled the room four times. Currently, Loran influences youth pastors and provides leadership at student conferences. He is on staff as the outreach leader at Renton Assembly and is making a difference. When Loran travels with me, he shares a leadership teaching called "What You Need to Do to Get a Guy Like Me to Work with You." It's how to involve the other "Lorans" who might be sitting in your church. You must have a vision that is worthy of their time.

Five Steps to Getting a Vision

It is a costly mistake to share a new vision without properly allowing the dream to burn within your heart. If you don't live and breathe the vision first, it doesn't matter how much you yell, how many banners you make, or how many times you mention it. No one else will get excited.

People will support a true vision. People know if it's burning in your heart or if it's just some idea you picked up at a conference. Before you open your mouth, make sure the vision is God-given, or else you will lose credibility. You won't lose credibility if you fail to reach a dream, but you will if you scream about a half-baked idea.

The following is a five-step process that I use to get a clear vision from God. This process takes some time, but when done correctly, it works.

1. Pray your vision

Some of the greatest dreams I have received were during prayer. God doesn't interrupt me; he simply gives me a thought or an idea. While you pray, ponder your vision. It sounds simple, yet if you miss this step, you will prevent the vision from getting deep within you. My simple rule is this: If I can't get excited about the vision when I pray, I won't get excited about it when I preach.

2. Write your vision

On a blank sheet of paper, write out your vision. Don't worry about where you should begin. Write what is on your mind. Even if it sounds crazy, write it out. Don't let past failures, opinions, present circumstances, or your busy schedule stop you from writing. Don't worry if the wording doesn't come out exactly right the first time—or even the second, third, or fourth attempt. Just write until you feel it. The bigger the vision the more times you will have to write it.

3. Think your vision

Think about your vision when you are working, on a date with your spouse, exercising, driving to work, and before you sleep. Many times, right before I close my eyes, I get up and hit DELETE on my keyboard. Lying there quietly, I realized that the vision was not the right direction.

Before I cast a vision publicly I think about it multiple times. I don't get in front of my church to read a banner. I share those thoughts that keep me up at night.

4. Talk your vision

Talking will help you to clarify your vision. Never cast your vision until you have discussed and confirmed it in private with people you trust. When I cast a vision, many people in the church have already heard me talk about it "accidentally." I watch their faces and learn whether to go forward with the vision or go back to the drawing board. The time to figure out your vision is not when you're standing in front of the church, but when you're looking someone in the face. If I get excited talking to you one-on-one, that excitement will translate authentically in public.

5. Review your vision

Pray, write, think, and talk about your vision again. Give it time to process and clarify by burning in your heart.

Five Ways to Cast Vision

If you can't cast vision, you will never grow a youth ministry. Vision casting is a skill. Most youth pastors know how to beg, use guilt, and complain. Few know how to stand before people and cast a vision that drives excitement and commitment. You may think some people in your church don't like your youth ministry. More likely, they just don't like the way your vision is being communicated.

1. Cast vision privately

After you have completed the five steps of getting a vision, you need to cast your vision privately to leaders. If you only cast it publicly, people will only think of your vision as a preaching tool.

My vision was to present the gospel to every student before they graduated from high school. Everyone knew it because I would talk about it while we were hanging out. It was who I was, not what I was trying to be.

2. Cast vision publicly

In ten years of youth ministry at Renton Assembly I never publicly asked people to get involved. However, I did cast the vision on every occasion.

> **Right in the middle of the message is a good time to talk about your vision.**

Right in the middle of the message is a good time to talk about your vision. If it's deep within you, you won't be able to stop it. Vision just leaks out.

Develop an annual vision-casting time with the church. The greatest day for me was the second Sunday of February. I would present the State of the Youth Ministry Address to the whole church. In 1996, I shared my five-year vision with the church. Wow! They caught it. The vision created enough enthusiasm to change a world. Every year, after sharing my vision, I had adults lined up to get involved.

Cast your vision when you give announcements. Don't wing it and mumble. *Think* about the vision behind the announcement. For example, if you are announcing a workday at church, tell people how they will be reaching their own community, "People notice if we value excellence. Let's reach this community together by showing up this Saturday to work."

3. Cast vision with passion

People follow leaders who have a deep passion. The vision has to be more than a slogan or some well thought out statements. Your vision must go from your head to your heart. Talk to any of my leaders. They know that I believe and live my dreams.

Your passion will come out when you pray, preach, and lead your ministry. Your passion is not something you can make up on the spot. Your passion will give you:

- *Desire* to begin the dream
- *Direction* to communicate the dream
- *Determination* to never give up on the dream
- *Discipline* to carry out the dream

4. Cast vision on purpose

Cast your vision by "accident" and on purpose. Develop strategic times throughout the year to cast it—at your house, over a cup of coffee, or just hanging out in the church lobby. Purposely cast your vision during leadership meetings, while giving announcements, in a Sunday school class, or while writing an article for your church newsletter.

Rule of thumb: Cast vision every thirty days—more, if necessary.

5. Cast vision with praise

The best time to affirm your vision is when someone does something that even remotely illustrates the heart of the vision. You get what you preach. If your vision is for students to learn how to worship, praise the students in your ministry who are worshiping God. Don't publicly stand before your students and bring undue attention to the students who are not worshiping God. If your vision is to reach more students with the gospel, shout when a student brings a friend to church. Shout about everything your students do right, instead of harping on everything they do wrong.

Fresh-Baked Cookies

I had a vision for every adult in our church to see themselves as ministers and use their everyday abilities to impact students. One day, Mickie Dickinson, a senior citizen at the church, wanted to get involved. I had no idea where to involve her, so she volunteered to bake cookies for our winter retreat. She did an outstanding job, and the students loved the cookies.

When I got back home to our church we had a testimony time. I paraded the changed lives before the church. The students shared what God had done for them personally. As I was leading the service I publicly and sincerely said to her, "Mickie, I want to thank you for coming to the retreat. Adults like you make a difference. You baked some cookies for our students. This was no big deal to you, but I want you to know that there are students here who are from broken homes and never get a fresh-baked cookie. Mickie, it is because of your cookie ministry that students were changed this weekend. You are the grandma that many students never had." On the next retreat, we got so many cookies we couldn't eat them all.

What did I do by praising Mickie?

- *Publicly,* I highlighted the details of the vision
- *Passionately,* I communicated the heart of the vision
- *Purposefully,* I reinforced the impact of the vision

You have to translate your vision in practical terms if you want people to follow it. You must show people how fresh-baked cookies can fulfill your vision.

---

12 Leadership Qualities of the Twenty-First Century Youth Pastor

Leaders chase after mentors.

Leaders grow daily.

Leaders have a clear vision.

Chapter 5

Why Do You Alone Sit as Judge?

Why do you alone sit as judge, while all these people stand around you from morning till evening? (Exodus 18:14b)

L eaders take responsibility.

Jethro kept asking Moses questions to help him think. First, he asked, "What is this you are doing for these people?" Then, a deeper question, "Why do you alone sit as judge?" If you don't have a team, you are not a strong leader. People won't follow if you can't be honest with yourself. Even God can't help a person who doesn't take full responsibility.

Before you can build a team, you must take responsibility for why you *don't* have a team. Don't hide behind some "spiritual" excuse, like you are the only one who can effectively minister to your students. Stop the excuses. You can do everything in this book, pray for God to send workers, and ask people to help until you are blue in the face. But if you don't change as a person, nothing will change around you.

The first step to change is honesty. Jethro asked Moses a question that forced him to face reality. Moses' response showed that he was more concerned about his own reputation than being honest. He got "spiritual" and said, "Because the people come to me to seek God's will . . ."

We are just like Moses, "God will bring them in. . . . My people are just not interested in youth ministry. . . . I am praying for leaders." Don't blame everyone else, including God, for ministering alone. God is not your problem. The church is not your problem. *You* are your problem.

Fifteen Reasons Why People Won't Work with You

1. People don't like you

Some youth pastors complain and actually convince themselves that people just don't like youth ministry. Be completely honest with yourself. People love God; they just don't like you. The most basic leadership principle in this book is: People only work with leaders they like. Learn to be likeable—smile, act like an adult, be polite, change your attitude. Whatever it takes, become a likeable person.

2. Your church is filled with leaders better than yourself

Is your church filled with adults who are responsible, who love their spouses, and who pay their bills on time? They won't work with someone who is irresponsible, has an unhealthy relationship with their spouse, and can't even handle the youth ministry budget. On a scale of 1 to 10, if your leadership is a 2, you will never recruit a leader who is a 3.

The solution? Personal growth. Go from being a 2 leader to a 3 leader, and then you will grow your leadership team. You may not think this is fair, but it is *reality*. Don't fight it. People will only follow you when you are a stronger leader than they are.

3. Your insecurity will not attract secure people

Here's why people don't like to work with insecure people: If they do something better than you, your poor feelings get hurt. Right now, there are people sitting in your church who can do a lot of things better than you. So what? Get over your insecurity and get them on your team.

I simply refuse to make decisions or provide leadership if there is an underlying motive of insecurity. I warn myself that it's not good and then say, "Troy, get a life. This person is probably as insecure as you are."

4. You do ministry alone

Every time you minister alone, you miss an opportunity to grow your team. Consider last week; how many things did you do alone? How many phone calls did you make alone? How many trips to the school campus did you take alone? How many students did you talk to without having an adult leader by your side? If you do ministry alone, you deserve to do ministry alone.

5. You don't take care of the leaders you have right now

Your leaders are your best advertising. Treat them like adults and you will be amazed at how many people will want to help with youth ministry. Think about it: Why would God give you more leaders if you don't take care of the ones you have?

6. You delegate as a way to get out of something

Leaders delegate so they can focus on ministry priorities, core values, and the vision of the youth ministry, not so they can get out of work. Leaders discover people's gifts and release them into ministry. Problems occur when you delegate things you don't like to do or are too lazy to try. A leader delegates to increase efficiency; a kid delegates because he is lazy. A leader delegates responsibility; a kid delegates to avoid responsibility.

> **A leader delegates to increase efficiency; a kid delegates because he is lazy.**

7. Your dream only attracts losers

Do you want strong leaders? You need a big dream. Only losers get excited about a fundraiser that won't make money. If you only have a handful of college students working with you, it might be because they haven't lived long enough to understand that you don't have a clue about leadership. Big dreams attract strong people. Small dreams attract small people. Create opportunities that are worthy of lifelong involvement and, who knows, maybe a busy person with great skills will give his or her time to your youth ministry.

8. Setting up chairs only goes so far

People want to do something significant for God. When an adult comes to you with incredible potential and their dreams of changing a world, don't tell them, "Prove yourself for three months by setting up chairs." Yes, everyone needs to be a servant. But if I can only set up chairs for you, I'm gone. People want to be *involved*. If you only offer meaningless tasks, they will find a person with a dream worth dying for. When you meet someone, begin looking for his or her gifts and passions. *Assume* they are gifted and called by God, because it's true. Then, help them discover their God-given potential.

9. You lack team-building skills

If you lack team-building skills, you will never have a team no matter how much you desire it. Learn how to build a team. A lack of skill in team building is the most common weakness in leaders today. We all talk team, but very few people live team. Without this basic skill, you will never lead a healthy youth ministry.

10. Your leadership meetings are a glorified Sunday school class

One of the main reasons adults don't work with youth pastors is that youth pastors often don't have a clue

> **High standards should be based on the leader's character, not on the leader's calendar.**

how to train and equip leaders. Leadership meetings that are thrown together at the last moment waste time and leave people unexcited about being a leader.

If you're not excited about your leadership meetings, no one else will be. If you don't take time to prepare and give your best, don't expect your leaders to give their best. Develop a leadership meeting that equips, empowers, and encourages your leaders. Create so much excitement for your leadership meetings that people in the church *ask* if they can be involved just so they can grow. (Details in chapter 11.)

11. You expect everybody to be the same

It is a mistake to expect everyone to commit the same amount of time and energy into your youth ministry. Quit bragging about all your high standards. High standards should be based on the leader's character, not on the leader's calendar. The standards should be based on how they are living, not how much time they are giving. If you only have one commitment level, you will *limit* the best leaders in your church. You need to create a leadership model that involves adults who can give different time and commitment levels.

12. You ask at the last minute

The people who say yes at the last minute either feel sorry for you or don't have a life. These are not the motivations that build a great team. That working mom with three little kids at home and the busy dad with work pressures will only say yes to being involved with your youth ministry if you ask them far in advance. The further in advance that you ask a person, the more likely it is they will say yes. This requires that you plan ahead. Think about your ministry needs three months in advance, rather than only three days in advance.

13. You look and talk too much like a youth pastor

At church, you can always tell who the youth pastor is. He or she hangs out with the students, looks like the students, can only talk about the youth ministry, and has no real adult friends. If you want adults to be involved with your ministry, you have to be an adult. Youth ministry is not some kind of permission to avoid maturity. Hang out with other adults and talk about something else besides your youth ministry. It's a good way to make sure you can relate to the real world.

14. You beg

In all my years of youth ministry I have never asked publicly for people to get involved. I have never said, "If you love God, you will work with students." The only thing I have done publicly is brag about my present leaders, cast vision, shout the praises of other ministries, and provide pastoral leadership to the people.

15. You think people read the bulletin

This may come as a shock to you: People don't read the bulletin. Leaders understand that people respond to vision, God-given leadership, and relationships. Your best leaders will join your team when they have a personal relationship with you, not when they read your insert in the bulletin. It's foolish to put a note in the bulletin and think, *If someone wants to help, they will respond.* This will not help you to build a team.

**12 Leadership Qualities of the
Twenty-First Century Youth Pastor**

Leaders chase after mentors.

Leaders grow daily.

Leaders have a clear vision.

Leaders take responsibility.

Chapter 6

Because the People Come to Me

Moses answered him, "Because the people come to me to seek God's will. Whenever they have a dispute, it is brought to me, and I decide between the parties and inform them of God's decrees and laws." (Exodus 18:15–16)

L eaders have a winning attitude.

A Jethro Experience always deals with the core attitudes. If someone tells you to change but doesn't deal with the unhealthy attitudes that caused the problem in the first place, you won't be able to truly change.

Moses became immediately defensive to leadership questions, like, "What is this you are doing? . . . Why do you alone sit as judge?"

How Moses responded gives insights into his inner attitudes about life and ministry. "Because the people come to me. I decide between the parties." He was deceived. Moses arrogantly believed that he was the only person who could minister to the people. In reality, he was the only obstacle to his own ministry. His successes, ideas, and agenda were more important to him than the people. Until you get over your pride you will never lead this generation effectively.

Great leaders are in tune with the right attitudes. Great leaders develop healthy perspectives in every aspect of their lives. What kind of attitude do you have? Is it dying, plateauing, or growing?

LEADERS

Dying	Plateauing	Growing
• Whining	• Wondering	• Winning attitude
• Has all the answers	• Has answers	• Asks questions
• My agenda	• Youth ministry agenda	• Church agenda
• Blind	• Nearsighted	• Farsighted
• Complains	• Compares	• Character
• Cares about reputation	• Cares about growth	• Cares about health
• Blames	• Excuses	• Evaluates

Eight Deadly Attitudes

A leader understands the power of having a healthy attitude. Everybody has attitudes that need to change. The best gifts, opportunities, and education won't make you an effective minister if your attitude is wrong.

1. Independence

An independent youth pastor says,

- "I don't need you"
- "I don't need the older generation"
- "I don't need other churches"
- "I don't need my denomination"
- "I don't need parental input"

This independent attitude will stop you from being effective in youth ministry. Your success will be limited because you won't be able to build a great team or grow as a leader. Imagine if Moses would have relied on an independent attitude. He would have said, "I am God's leader. I don't need you, Jethro." But Moses *did* need Coach Jethro. Be careful, success is the breeding ground of independent attitudes.

2. Ungratefulness

"You owe me something." Here is what many youth pastors consider a hard workday.

9:30 A.M.	—	Arrive at office
10:00 A.M.	—	Begin work
11:00 A.M.	—	Lunch (hang with other discouraged youth pastors and complain)
1:00 P.M.	—	Back to the office (had to pray with youth pastors)
1:30 P.M.	—	Check e-mail
2:30 P.M.	—	Do some work
4:00 P.M.	—	Hard day (need to leave early)

It's easy to take ministry for granted. Why don't you quit and get a secular job for a while? It will destroy any ungrateful attitudes you have. Try working a job that has a 6:00 A.M. wake-up, an ungodly boss, late nights, commuter traffic, and only an *hour* for lunch. Too many college graduates expect churches to pay them big bucks when they apply for their first job at the age of 22. If that's you, be ashamed. You have to *prove* yourself. There is no red carpet. Grow up and learn that real ministry is not about *you* at all.

When the senior pastor takes you out for lunch, try paying the bill occasionally. Say thank-you if the church gives you a Christmas bonus. Work more than a full day. If you do, maybe someone will pay you

Because the People Come to Me

what you are worth. And if you're tempted to complain, think about what else you could be doing for a living.

3. Arrogance

"You should listen to me. I have been alive for 25 years. I have the answers." Trust me, you don't. If you did, you wouldn't be talking about great things, you would be doing them. Anyone can talk, but leaders *do*.

Moses was the most humble leader in the Bible. Humility is exactly what made him great. His Jethro Experience mandated a humble attitude.

An arrogant attitude makes God sick and it gets in the way of ministry. A true leader is humble before God and has no problem keeping his or her mouth shut until the appropriate time to speak. If you lose credibility when you speak, your opinions on how to do things will never be considered. Don't focus only on yourself. You'll miss great opportunities to lead and have a positive influence on others.

4. Either-Or Attitude

"My way is the only way." Only children fight and demand their own way. Parents discipline children for this kind of behavior. Leaders create win-win situations.

The church is struggling with this in all types of ways. Some pastors say, "We are a seeker-sensitive church. Get rid of all the church traditions. Everything you do should be for the seeker."

> **Leaders create win-win situations.**

Other pastors say, "We are a revival church. God moves here." Leaders understand that God wants both kinds of churches, not just one or the other. Leaders work to find a winning solution for as many people as possible.

Don't put the following people in an either-or situation:

- *Senior pastor.* Don't ever say to him, "Either you like my idea, or you're not creative."
- *Board.* Don't ever say, "I have heard from God. Why are you hesitating?"
- *Parents.* Don't ever say, "Either your students come every week, or they can't be involved."
- *Leaders.* Don't ever say, "If you can't make it this Sunday morning, you really aren't a committed leader."

5. Insecurity

"Please give me attention." Ministers are some of the most insecure people on the face of the earth. Insecure people attract more insecure people.

I remember going as a young minister to my first District Council, a gathering with hundreds of other denominational ministers. I walked in and thought, *No one knows me, and no one is talking to me.* My insecurity was louder than my logic. I went into the restroom and looked in the mirror and said, "Troy, be a leader. Stop blaming everybody. If you want to talk to someone, go find someone."

To be a great leader, you must deal with your own insecurity. Imagine how insecure Moses felt when Jethro started giving him advice. A Jethro Experience requires that you overcome insecurity and grow.

6. Defensiveness

"It's not my fault." Actually, it probably is your fault; and if you maintain a defensive attitude, you will never grow. Leaders take responsibility for their actions; they pay the price. A healthy attitude is one that takes responsibility quickly, rather than placing blame. Stop blaming your church if your youth ministry isn't growing. Stop blaming your

Because the People Come to Me

students if they don't hunger after God. Stop blaming your secretary if things aren't completed on time. Blaming hinders you from understanding the real issues. People may say,

- "My church is too big"
- "My church is too small"
- "I am too young"
- "I am too old"
- "My senior pastor doesn't give input"
- "My senior pastor micro manages everything"
- "My community is too small"
- "My community is huge"
- "My students have too much church background"
- "My students have no foundation"
- "I don't have enough time because I am part time"
- "People won't be involved with youth ministry because I am full time"
- "The last leader made some big mistakes"
- "It's so hard to follow a great leader"

Leaders quickly admit that they need to grow. Then they take full responsibility for the condition of their youth ministry.

7. Comparison

"I am better than you." If you think you are better than someone because you have fifty kids in your ministry and they have forty-five, get a life. Comparisons will destroy you as a leader in two ways.

1. Someone will always be doing ministry "worse" than you. If you're not careful, pride will ruin your life by making you complacent when you should be growing as a leader.

2. Someone will always be doing ministry "better" than you. Comparing yourself to them causes frustration and discouragement, not success.

I don't compare one message to another message, one event to another, or one success to another success. Comparisons will hinder you from being an effective leader. Give your best ideas and energy to every event you are doing right now. Don't try to beat last year. It will hinder you from enjoying this year.

> **Comparisons will hinder you from being an effective leader.**

After one service at a 5,000-student youth conference, someone made a comparison, "The drama was not as good as last year." Hmm, students were saved, filled with the Holy Spirit, and mobilized into effective ministry, and all he could talk about was how it compared to last year's drama?

Work now. Enjoy now. Rejoice in what God *is* accomplishing today. Don't waste your time comparing anything to someone else's ministry or yesterday's successes.

8. Clueless

"What's wrong with me?" This is the scariest attitude to see in a youth pastor. You're in trouble if you have a bad attitude and you don't even know it. If you accept a terrible attitude in yourself, there is no hope for you. I would have more hope for an arrogant youth pastor who at least knows there's a problem. Leaders recognize unhealthy attitudes. They know when they are defensive, critical, arrogant, or blaming someone. If you don't know, get help so you can grow and build a team. The last thing you want is for the students to pick up your insecurity, arrogance, defensiveness, or any unhealthy attitude you may have.

The following are some questions that help me to honestly examine my motives. Answer these questions and reflect on them. It's important to be honest with yourself.

- Why do I feel like I don't need people?
- Am I making this decision for the right reason?
- What is my attitude toward my senior pastor? Why do I feel I can grow this church better than he can?
- Why do I prepare messages at the last moment? What attitude does this reflect?
- Why do I treat my spouse with disrespect?
- Why do I struggle with my prayer life? What does this say about my attitude toward God?
- Why can't I save money? What is my attitude toward my finances?
- Do I want to preach on a Sunday morning for the church's benefit or my personal gain?
- Why do I enjoy people comparing me to my children's pastor?

The Attitude That Saved Me

One of the first of many youth pastor mistakes I made was at the age of 22. I was excited about taking a bunch of students to Ocean Shores, Washington. I knew how to lead a trip—I graduated from Northwest College. So, with more energy than wisdom, I didn't bother asking for advice.

That day, 80 young people showed up. I had one bus. *No problem! We will just use several cars.* So I got 20 leaders with cars and said, "We all have to stay together. I am in the van. Follow me."

Everyone was lost before we got out of the parking lot. On the freeway, I thought, *Where is everybody? They don't follow my leadership.*

Worse yet, I decided to change plans and stop in Olympia for a McDonald's break. With a brilliant idea on how to tell all 20 vehicles which exit ramp to get off, I asked the students in my van, "Who wants to stand on the side of I-5 and wave down vehicles?"

Any 15-year-old would say, "Me! I will!" Was I involving students in ministry? No, I was being a dumb youth pastor. Picture two 15-year-old students standing on I-5, waving for a bus and 20 cars. I waited at McDonald's all by myself. *Nobody* showed up. And when I went back to pick up the two students, they weren't there. So, I continued on to Ocean Shores. I was worried but kept thinking someone had to have picked them up. It would be normal for someone to just stop on I-5 and pick up two teenagers, right?

I got to Ocean Shores and all the vehicles were there. "Did anyone pick up two young people on the side of I-5?" Everyone just laughed, thinking I was joking. No one had seen them.

I jumped back in the van and started racing back to Olympia, crying, *Mercy, what am I doing? I just killed two young people.* (They don't teach you how to handle that at Northwest College.) I decided it would be better to go to the Ocean Shores Police Station. I walked in, introduced myself, and explained the situation. The policeman stared at me. "Now, you're trying to tell us you left two young people on the side of I-5? And you are a minister?" I confessed and begged for help. The officers made some calls and finally informed me that the police in Olympia had picked them up. I had made a tragic mistake, but I thanked God that everything had ended up fine.

> # Mercy, what am I doing? I just killed two young people.

As a kid youth pastor, I had a lot to learn in order to lead students. The moment I got home, I called the parents and my senior pastor and said, "I blew it." There were no excuses; I took full responsibility for my stupidity.

You want to know why I was able to stay at one church for ten years? You want to know why Renton Assembly followed my leadership?

Because I was willing to admit when I was wrong. When I made mistakes, I didn't make excuses. I learned, grew, and *changed.*

**12 Leadership Qualities of the
Twenty-First Century Youth Pastor**

Leaders chase after mentors.

Leaders grow daily.

Leaders have a clear vision.

Leaders take responsibility.

Leaders have a winning attitude.

Chapter 7

What You Are Doing Is Not Good

Moses father-in-law replied, "What you are doing is not good. You and these people who come to you will only wear yourselves out. The work is too heavy for you; you cannot handle it alone." (Exodus 18:17–18)

L eaders reinvent themselves.

Imagine this: Moses just delivered the Israelites out of Egyptian bondage. He just divided the Red Sea. Everything was great. Then, Moses' mentor and coach looked at him and said, "What you are doing is not good."

Moses could have responded with a cynical attitude:

- "Jethro, you don't know what you're talking about."
- "What have you ever done in ministry?"
- "I have just delivered the Israelites out of bondage. Who have you helped?"
- "You're too old. You're not in touch with this generation."

Likewise, when your youth ministry is growing and you're feeling good, some old minister may say, "What you are doing is not good." Listen to him. A Jethro Experience will either destroy you or grow you. You choose to either get defensive or reinvent yourself. Whenever your mentor says, "What you are doing is not good," make a choice to be a leader, not a defensive kid. You haven't been ministering long enough if you haven't gone through the painful experience of change.

> Moses told his father-in-law about everything the LORD had done to Pharaoh and the Egyptians for Israel's sake and about all the hardships they had met along the way and how the LORD had saved them. (Exodus 18:8)

Moses hid behind God's successes by talking too much. He didn't realize his own ministry had changed. Moses just kept doing the same thing over again. He got up, people stood around him from morning until evening, he answered questions, preached, responded to all the e-mails, and planned all of tomorrow's activities.

Your greatest enemy in leadership can be yourself.

Your greatest enemy in leadership can be yourself. Your gifts, war stories, and experiences are the very things that can keep you from growing. Leaders understand that just because something worked yesterday doesn't mean that it will work today. They are always asking, "How can I make continuous improvements? . . . What changes do I need to make? . . . Is it time to reinvent this idea?"

Leonard Sweet said, "Postmodern culture is a change or be changed world. The word is out: Reinvent yourself for the twenty-first century or die. Some would rather die than change." *

---

* Leonard Sweet, *Soul Tsunami: Sink or Swim in New Millennium Culture* (Grand Rapids: Zondervan, 1999) p. 75.

Seven Indicators That You Need to Reinvent Yourself

1. The good is robbing you of the best

What you are doing is not good. (Exodus 18:17)

Don't allow good things to rob you of the *best*. Don't waste your time trying to impress other youth pastors or leaders. Moses did good things. In fact, he probably could be the keynote speaker in today's conferences. He could share a lot of insight on how to deliver students out of bondage. But Moses allowed "good" things to rob him of the "best" things. He did everything by himself and neglected his own personal growth and development. He sacrificed his family for his ministry by allowing the urgent to override the important.

The Millennials will define the twenty-first century. William Strauss, one of the foremost experts on this generation, said, "Pick the poison: pot, alcohol, other mind-altering drugs, cigarettes, teen sex. If the Millennials ultimately decide that any or all of these are acceptable behavior, that choice will resonate deeply throughout twenty-first century America."* Good intentions and good programs will fall short with this generation. If you are allowing the good to rob you of the best, reinvent yourself today.

2. You're worn out

You . . . will only wear yourselves out. (Exodus 18:18)

If you weren't the youth pastor at your church, would you be involved with your ministry? Being tired and weary is one of the first signs that you must reinvent yourself. Something may be wrong with the way you are doing ministry. I am not referring to physical fatigue; there are

---

* William Strauss and Neil Howe, "The Battle for the Millennial Generation", The Fourth Turning: Discussions (November 24, 1997). http://www.fourthturning.com (April 23, 2000).

times you just need to sleep, not reinvent your whole schedule. I am talking about being worn out emotionally, spiritually, and mentally.

You need to reinvent yourself if you:

- Have lost your passion for youth ministry
- Are not even excited about showing up to your next youth event
- Dread the thought of preparing another lesson

I am sick and tired of seeing youth pastors who are sick and tired. Why is it that every time there is a leadership training conference, it seems the only thing we do is pray and complain about our schedules, ministries, and the undue stress in our lives? Instead of a pity party, we need a priority party. We need someone to share insights on how to change. Notice that Jethro didn't say to Moses, "I feel sorry for you. Your situation must be difficult. Let's pray for your stress." No, Jethro told Moses to grow up, do ministry differently, and learn new skills.

> **A whole generation of students is going to hell, and all we do is complain about the misery of ministering to them.**

A whole generation of students is going to hell, and all we do is complain about the misery of ministering to them. The Millennials are the most optimistic generation to ever live. Eighty percent describe themselves as excited about life.[*] Four out of five say that they are optimistic about the future. According to *Newsweek*, "Today's teens are infused with an optimism not seen among kids in decades."[†] The Millennials want a leader who is equally infused with optimism and excitement about the future.

---

[*] Thom S. Rainier, *The Bridger Generation* (Nashville: Broadman & Holman Publishers, 1997) p. 18.
[†] Sharon Begley, "A World of Their Own", *Newsweek* (May 8, 2000) p. 54–56.

3. Your people are worn out

> You and these people who come to you will only wear yourselves out. (Exodus 18:18)

Are students and leaders in your youth ministry bored, unmotivated, or worn out? If so, you need to reinvent yourself. If a program is draining the energy, reinvent the program. If you have to drum up excitement about a program or event, this is a good indication it is time to rethink it. Enthusiasm is contagious; dry programs are draining.

The Millennials want to make a difference in the world. Nine out of ten believe it *is* possible for one person to make a significant impact.

Enthusiasm is contagious.

Nearly a third of the people working on any Habitat for Humanity project are under the age of 25.* The Millennials have an inborn civic virtue. Do you? If your youth ministry is not involving them and providing a place to make a difference, change.

4. You are doing ministry alone

> The work is too heavy for you; you cannot handle it alone. (Exodus 18:18)

The work is too heavy for you. You can't handle it alone. If you are doing ministry alone, this is an indication that you need to begin changing the way you do ministry. The Millennials value teamwork. William Strauss wrote, "This is much more a team-playing generation. Boomers may be bowling alone, but Millennials are playing soccer in teams."† You will not reach this generation unless you redefine teamwork.

The Millennials respond to adults who are authentic and truly love them. They don't respond to a title or position. They don't respect the

---

* George Barna, *Third Millennium*, The Barna Research Group, Ltd. (1999) p. 38.
† William Strauss and Neil Howe, "The Battle for the Millennial Generation".

word *pastor*, but they'll trust someone who cares enough to spend time with them—a win-win situation. By yourself, you can only love so many students. Your responsibility is to develop an authentic, adult leadership team that truly loves students.

5. You have no one coaching you

Imagine if Moses didn't have Jethro there to coach him? What would have happened to his life and ministry? It was Coach Jethro who made Moses come to grips with his need to reinvent himself. Strong leaders seek out people who won't just pat them on the back and say, "Good job." They find leaders who are stronger than themselves and coaches who will bring out their best.

If no one is coaching or mentoring you, this is a strong indication that you need to reinvent yourself.

6. You are too busy to grow

You can no longer depend on games and icebreakers. Students want a leader, not a new program. According to Barna Research, relationships bring students to church and substance persuades them to return. One study revealed that learning practical and credible insights about God was the most important reason some people returned to a particular church.[*]

Studies show that today's teens are the most occupationally and educationally ambitious generation ever.[†] Three-quarters say they will definitely attend college after graduating from high school.[††] The twenty-first century youth pastor must be occupationally and educationally ambitious to grow in order to effectively lead students. You had better make time to read books, think, and prepare your messages.

---

[*] Barna, *Third Millennium*, p. 55.
[†] Begley, "A World of Their Own", p. 55.
[††] Barna, *Third Millennium*, p. 35.

7. Your youth ministry is not growing

Leaders understand that healthy ministries grow naturally. If your youth ministry is not growing, it's a health issue, not a program issue.

One third of the Millennials attend a Protestant youth group in America.* Twenty-two million teens are associated with a Christian youth

The Millennials are interested in spiritual things.

group.† Sixty-seven percent of students pray to God on any given day.†† The Millennials are interested in spiritual things. They are searching for God. There are thousands of students *ready* to get saved. There are thousands looking for a community and healthy relationships. No single program can help you. No idea will solve all your problems. Become a leader who can adapt and lead students to the Promised Land.

Five Deadly Assumptions

Moses just assumed that everything was great. His youth ministry looked good to most people. Unfortunately, Moses assumed what had worked yesterday would work today.

Leaders question their own assumptions on a daily basis. If you assume that everything is going great, you will never change.

1. It worked in my teen years

Many youth pastors just repeat what their youth pastor did when they were a student. Leaders can set aside their own experiences, desires, and agendas to provide what's best for their students. Who cares what you liked when you were a teenager? Wake up! Those ministries are irrelevant for this generation.

---

* Barna, *Third Millennium*, p. 40.
† Ibid., p. 41.
†† Ibid., p. 29.

What You Are Doing Is Not Good

2. It worked five years ago

Change happens quickly in our society. The Millennials are grow-ing up in a world that changes and can even revolutionize itself in five years. Every day, I begin my ministry again. Every day, I have to ask,

- "What is God saying?"
- "What does this generation need today?"
- "How has this generation changed?"

The Millennials will experience more changes than any previous generation. You will not make it in youth ministry if you just repeat what makes you the most comfortable. If you don't change the way you do ministry, you will be obsolete in three to five years. Every day, the rules of youth ministry change again. Don't just repeat daily schedules and do ministry the same.

I have a three-to-five-year rule in youth ministry. When considering using a program I've used before, I ask, "If I started today with this program, how would it look? What would I do different?" I may not need to throw the whole program away. I may just need to reinvent the vision of the program in my heart and soul.

3. It worked last year

Don't look at your calendar in order to repeat what you did last year. Everything should be honestly evaluated every time it is done. The old slogan is: "If you do the same things, you will get the same results." That's not true anymore. In today's ministry, if you do the same things you did even a year ago, you may get a completely different result. Last year's success may not work this year. Conduct an honest evaluation. Is it time to totally reinvent this program? Is it time to get rid of it? What changes would make it more effective?

4. It works in that other community

When people try to sell their programs or youth ministry ideas, I get nervous. We like to think our own solutions would work globally. Yes, new ideas and programs can be good, but *principles* are what make the difference. Leaders are people of principle. They retain the principles behind the programs so they can adapt them to their own community.

When you hear a great idea or concept, ask yourself if it can be adapted to your situation. Don't ask, "How can I adopt this?" If it doesn't work, it will discourage you faster than anything else. Don't allow the enemy to have that opportunity. Remember, students and churches are different in every community and region.

5. It works for that other leader

Every leader has individual gifts and callings. We are all unique. If God uses you differently than someone else, it doesn't mean you are less valuable—or any more important. This kind of game has been played way too long. Ask God to show you how and what *you* need to do to become a better leader.

Longevity in Youth Ministry

Longevity is vital in youth ministry. Without longevity you can't have an impact in student's lives. The Millennials won't trust a short-term youth pastor. However, don't use longevity and experience as excuses for stagnation. There is a big difference between ten years of youth ministry experience and one year repeated ten times. We live in a change or be-changed world.

> **The Millennials won't trust a short-term youth pastor.**

Yesterday's ideas or yesterday's anointing won't work. Don't assume you are being effective, especially if deep down inside you know something is wrong. It is deadly to rely on those assumptions. Students don't need a new program; they need a new leader.

The Difference between *Change* and *Compromise*

Don't confuse change with compromise. Leaders understand that compromise allows a worldly spirit to creep into the ministry. This is evident when students are entertained more than encouraged to grow spiritually.

Too many youth pastors panic when society begins to change. They revise their programs before reviewing their leadership. The kid youth pastor, without knowing it, compromises standards all in the name of change. Do not compromise solid biblical principles in order to minister to students. The Millennials want high standards; they are willing to commit their lives to a cause bigger than they are.

---

12 Leadership Qualities of the Twenty-First Century Youth Pastor

Leaders chase after mentors.

Leaders grow daily.

Leaders have a clear vision.

Leaders take responsibility.

Leaders have a winning attitude.

Leaders reinvent themselves.

Chapter 8

You Must

Listen now to me and I will give you some advice, and may God be with you. You must be the people's representative before God and bring their disputes to him. Teach them the decrees and laws, and show them the way to live and the duties they are to perform. (Exodus 18:19–20)

L eaders understand what they must do.

This was the moment in Moses' life that he had to decide whether or not to be a leader. Jethro looked straight into Moses' eyes and said, "Listen to me." Moses had to go back to school. The University of Jethro was going to speak. If he passed the test, Moses would save the nation of Israel. If he skipped class, he would lose his ministry.

Jethro gave Moses a personal growth plan with five steps. It was a practical plan that he could follow. When your mentor says, "I will give you some advice," listen. If you need your mentor to hit you over the head and say, "Do this or you will be fired," you are not teachable. Jethro had wisdom. He gave advice, but Moses had to decide what to do with it. Advice from someone wiser than you is priceless.

Moses' Personal Growth Plan

1. Pray

> You must be the people's representative before God and bring their disputes to him. (Exodus 18:19)

The first step to Moses' personal growth plan was prayer. Moses was so busy ministering to the people that he didn't have time to pray. Great leaders know how to get a hold of God. You can't delegate your prayer life. It sounds basic, but every once in a while we need someone to say, "This is a Bible. Open it. This is prayer. Pray."

Every great leader will neglect prayer at one point or another. It's easy to get busy doing the ministry and forget the one who called you into ministry. Jethro knew that Moses was depending on his personal wisdom more than God's wisdom. Jethro said, "Bring their disputes to him"—to God. Instead of worrying about students' problems, bring them to God. Don't work yourself to death to solve every problem. This may surprise you, but God is quite capable of working in their lives without you.

You can't delegate your prayer life.

Extremes are common in Christian leaders. Some pray all the time and never work on new skills. Others work hard, learn new skills, and never pray. Both extremes are ineffective. You can't lead effectively unless you work hard *and* pray hard. One of my personal ministry slogans is: "Early to bed, early to rise. Pray against hell and advertise."

2. Teach

> Teach them the decrees and laws. (Exodus 18:20)

The second part of Moses' personal growth plan was to grow his speaking, teaching, and equipping skills. Moses was so busy ministering to people that he didn't have time to focus on teaching and preaching.

Preach the Word. Teach students the decrees and laws, not fads and opinions. This generation is hungry. Be creative and use illustrations. The focus of your message should always be biblically based, complementing the Word. Do not use the Word to complement your great illustrations. For a message to have impact, its very core must be the Word of God.

Your responsibility is to equip God's people for works of service. You will never have a strong team if you can't equip them with the proper skills to lead. Don't involve someone without equipping him or her first. If you do that, you will lose your best leaders.

3. Lead by example

> ... and show them the way to live and the duties they are to perform. (Exodus 18:20)

Leaders understand the power of an example. Developing your character must be part of your personal growth plan. You must live with character. You must *show* people how to live before you tell them how to live. No matter how great of a communicator you are, people will follow your actions more than your words. Your greatest communication tool is your life.

Integrity in leadership is not an option. You will die without character. If you only become a better leader and not a better person, you will limit your leadership ability.

Here are some rules that will help you protect your character for life.

Ten Commandments for Youth Ministry

1. Thou shall not spend time alone with any student of the opposite sex.
2. Thou shall not take home or visit any student of the opposite sex while alone.

3. Thou shall not inappropriately touch or show affection to any student.
4. Thou shall not discuss sexual issues one-on-one with any student of the opposite sex. Refer them.
5. Thou shall carbon copy (CC) your spouse or a responsible adult when e-mailing any student of the opposite sex.
6. Thou shall not view anything on the Internet that you would not watch without your spouse present.
7. Thou shall not discuss your marriage problems with any student.
8. Thou shall not counsel any student of the opposite sex alone. Refer them.
9. Thou shall keep your office door open when anyone of the opposite sex is present.
10. Thou shall use wisdom when praying for, ministering to, and showing appreciation to any student of the opposite sex.

4. Build a team

The work is too heavy for you. You cannot handle it alone. (Exodus 18:18)

The most important part of Moses' personal growth plan was learning to build a team. Why don't we have more youth ministries running 500 or 1,000 students? Why are most churches less than 100 people? Is it because their pastors don't pray or don't have good hearts? No, you can pray, have a good heart, and live a godly life and still never grow a youth ministry. Don't say, "God help me grow my ministry." Instead, say, "God help me grow my *team*." If you grow a team, you will have so many young people you won't be able to control them. Pray all you want, but if you can't work with a team, you will not grow. Love them all you want—and those 30 students might love you—but that will never grow your youth ministry.

Jethro gave Moses three practical steps to building a team. Any youth pastor who follows these steps and personally grows will develop a leadership team.

Step 1: Select capable people

> But select capable men from all the people. (Exodus 18:21)

There are countless adults in your church who are waiting for a leader to follow.

A leader knows how to select capable people, connect with adults in the church, and can see every person as a future leader. Stop making excuses that there is nobody at your church to help with youth ministry. People avoid you because that is all you complain about. There are countless adults in your church who are waiting for a leader to follow.

Step 2: Appoint them as leaders

> Appoint them as officials over thousands, hundreds, fifties, and tens. (Exodus 18:21)

After you recognize the potential in the adults of your church, put them on a team. The leader develops a leadership team model that involves everybody. This model involves people who can give one hour a day or even just one hour a year. It says yes to every willing adult in the church.

Step 3: Have them serve

> Have them serve as judges for the people at all times. (Exodus 18:22)

Strong leaders don't sit around and watch the preaching on Wednesday night. The adults in your church who can add value and credibility to your leadership team want to be involved. Let them serve, or they will quit.

5. Learn new skills

The final part of Moses' personal growth plan was that he had to learn new skills. Jethro communicated to Moses all types of new skills: team building, communication, listening, empowerment of people, and organization. You will not survive in the twenty-first century without a fundamental commitment to learning new skills. Leading students takes more than just a good heart; you must understand how to grow, develop, and learn new skills.

Christians tend to get nervous when you suggest that skills are ministry essentials. They get mystical and say, "God builds His church." Yes, but *how* does God build His church? He does it through people. If you lack the necessary skills to build his church, you limit the kingdom of God.

Some people grow spiritually but don't have a clue how to work with others or motivate themselves. We need to grow spiritually and in new skills. It's not an either-or proposition.

I just recently had a well-meaning minister say to me, "You probably read all of those leadership books."

I responded with confidence, "Yes, and that's why people follow me. What about you?"

Think of aviation. Would you fly with a pilot who loves God but doesn't have experience with commercial airlines? Or would you prefer to fly with an atheist who has 20 years of experience? I'd fly with the skilled pilot, whether he cusses or not.

There are five skills that youth pastors must master in the twenty-first century. These skills are:

1. Vision casting
2. Team building

3. Mastering their midweek—providing a successful celebration service for students
4. Growing students
5. Reaching students

These skills can be observed, learned, and developed. If you are hungry to grow, you can learn them. But the learning will only begin when you desire and hunger for it. Learning new skills starts the moment you recognize that you must grow.

---

12 Leadership Qualities of the Twenty-First Century Youth Pastor

Leaders chase after mentors.

Leaders grow daily.

Leaders have a clear vision.

Leaders take responsibility.

Leaders have a winning attitude.

Leaders reinvent themselves.

Leaders understand what they must do.

Chapter 9

But Select
Capable Men

But select capable men from all the people—men who fear God, trustworthy men who hate dishonest gain—and appoint them as officials over thousands, hundreds, fifties, and tens. (Exodus 18:21)

He chose capable men from all Israel. . . . (Exodus 18:25)

L eaders involve everyone in ministry.

Envision what Moses was going through at this point. Jethro had just told him he wasn't being productive. He spoke right to his situation, "You are only wearing yourself out." Then Jethro told him that he must grow himself as a man of God and as a leader. Jethro helped Moses understand his own vision, his attitude, and why people didn't want to work with him.

After Jethro rearranged the priorities and daily schedule, Moses had to wrestle with the questions, "How do I empower a team? Where do I begin?"

Jethro answered, "Moses, look around you. Choose capable leaders from all the people." The first step to building a leadership team is opening your eyes and see the potential in everybody around you.

Select capable men from all the people. (Exodus 18:21)

Deprogram yourself to only recognize a particular type of person for youth ministry. A leader sees ministry potential in everybody. Don't limit yourself to adults who have a lot of time on their hands. The people who will help you build a great youth ministry may have many other commitments in life. Trust me, the miracles are in the house. Your future leaders are already attending your church. Begin training yourself to recognize everyone as a future leader.

As a young youth pastor, I attended a workshop on recruiting a youth staff. The speaker was very proud of the expectations and rigid processes he had for joining his leadership team. I don't know if Jesus would have qualified. I guarantee the speaker wasn't doing all those things personally. I thought, *Nobody in my church qualifies. This guy just disqualified my best leaders.* Parents couldn't be involved because of their youth, senior citizens were too old—and the list went on.

At the end of the workshop, he said proudly, "And I only have six staff, but they are good."

I thought, *You will never build a great youth ministry with this kind of limited thinking.*

Characteristics of a Healthy Leadership Team

A healthy leadership team involves all types of adults with all types of life experiences. Honestly evaluate your leadership team. Is it truly healthy? To be sure it's healthy, you need to include adults who:

- Are in their twenties, thirties, forties, fifties, and even senior citizens
- Are from solid Christian homes and those who are from broken homes

- Have served God all of their lives and those who are new Christians
- Have great marriages and those who have walked through a difficult divorce but are still serving God
- Can give one hour a day and those who can give one hour a year
- Can handle multiple responsibilities and those who only want one task

Your future leaders are already attending your church.

- Enjoy loving students and those who enjoy working behind the scenes
- You enjoy being around and those you don't
- Are gifted in leadership and those who are gifted in helps
- Are single and those who are married
- Have attended your church for years and those who have just started to attend

How to Connect with Adults

Be careful to avoid the youth ministry "bubble." You know you are in the bubble if you are only hanging out with students and aren't spending healthy interaction time with adults. You will never build an adult leadership team if you only connect with students.

Here are eight ways to connect with adults in your church.

1. Meet people in the church lobby

Get to church early Sunday morning and meet the adults before and after services. Stop preparing messages at the last minute and get out in the lobby to connect. There is incredible power in a face-to-face interaction. If you hide in your office, you don't deserve to have adults help you out in your ministry.

2. Take a potential leader out

When an adult shows up to your youth service, they are sending a loud message that they are interested in youth ministry. If you don't take the time, you will lose them. When an adult shows up, invite them out that night. Build that relationship and secure a potential leader.

3. Use the hit-and-run effect

When you meet a sharp young couple with two kids, don't come out and say, "Would you like to be involved with our youth ministry on Sundays, Wednesdays, during annual retreats, and with our weekly phone ministry?"

Try the hit-and-run approach by gently saying, "There are areas in your life that would be great with our youth ministry. Let's talk sometime." You hit the subject and then run, giving the people time to process the idea. Be careful not to get labeled as the youth pastor who always needs something. Leaders know when they are being too pushy. You must become an expert on people.

> **Leaders see potential in people when no one else can.**

4. Keep your eyes open

Always search your church for potential leaders who can help out. The greatest leaders I've had were adults you wouldn't expect. I would talk to them on Sunday morning or run into them at a restaurant. Leaders see potential in people when no one else can.

5. Be involved with the life of the church

A kid youth pastor is only involved with the youth ministry. A leader is involved with the *life* of the church. He or she shows up to help in the children's ministry, music productions, and church workdays. These are great times to connect with adults who have nothing (yet) to do with the youth ministry.

6. Connect with your church from the pulpit

When you have the opportunity to pray in the service, give announcements, or preach, connect with adults by caring for the whole church. If the music ministry has an outreach, be the one to cast the vision for it. If the children's ministry has an upcoming activity, get excited about it.

Your adults will connect with the youth ministry when they connect with you.

Connect with your adults by preaching like a pastor. Many youth pastors act and talk so much like youth pastors that it's no wonder senior pastors hesitate to hand over the microphone. In fact, he may be doing you a favor. If you are given the opportunity to preach, don't mention the youth ministry at first. Don't beg for workers. Your adults will connect with the youth ministry when they connect with you.

7. Hang out with adults

Learn how to "hang" with adults beyond the context of youth ministry. Responsible adults will not work with you if you don't know how to interact with them. Make it a habit to schedule time in an adult environment.

8. Conduct yourself as a pastor

You are called to be a pastor to students, not a youth pastor who lacks an appropriate concept of everything around you. The Millennials will follow leaders who are authentic and real. Many youth pastors look ridiculous. It's obvious they are trying too hard, and that can be a turn-off to students. Students really want you to be *you*. Think, dress, and conduct yourself as a pastor.

High Expectations

... men who fear God, trustworthy men who hate dishonest gain. (Exodus 18:21)

Outline clear expectations for everyone on your leadership team. Be sure your expectations are well thought out, clearly communicated, and flexible in nature. Here are some basic principles to keep in mind when developing expectations.

- *Be more concerned with a leader's character than his calendar.* Find leaders who fear God and who are trustworthy.
- *Keep expectations simple.* Limit yourself to five clear expectations. If you can't remember your expectations or what they entail, you have too many or they are too complicated.
- *Have different expectations.* Not everyone on your team should require the same expectations. Put higher expectations on directors and youth staff than the support team. I will discuss in detail the different youth ministry teams and their expectations and responsibilities.

Five Expectations I Had for My Youth Ministry Team

1. *Faithful to God*

Every leader must be faithful to God. Your leaders must live a life above reproach in every area. They must live the example you want to set for every student. You want leaders who love God, live with integrity, and believe in students. However, no leader is perfect. They can and do make mistakes. Don't wait for people to walk on water before you let them wait on tables.

2. Faithful to the life of the local church

Youth ministry is only one part of the local church. Your leaders must be faithful in attendance and must financially support the church.

3. Faithful to their ministry

The goal of every leader is to find a ministry and fulfill it. Your role is to help your leaders discover their God-given gifts and strengths. This is an ongoing process; it takes a lifetime but is worth the journey.

> **Don't wait for people to walk on water before you let them wait on tables.**

4. Faithful to leadership meetings

One of the most important expectations I had for my leaders was attending the leadership meetings. Those meetings were designed for personal growth, encouragement, and vision casting. (Details in chapter 11.)

5. Faithful to the youth ministry

Depending on the responsibilities and roles involved, being faithful to the youth ministry can play itself out differently for different people. All of your leaders need to be committed to the vision and strategy of the youth ministry.

Ten People to Involve in Youth Ministry

. . . from all the people. (Exodus 18:21)

Jethro told Moses to select capable people "from all the people." When youth pastors say, "I don't have any leaders," they are really saying they can't motivate and train the countless number of adults sitting in church every Sunday morning. Quit making excuses.

Simple leadership rule: Involve everyone, everywhere, every time. Anytime you make up a reason why you can't involve a group of people, you limit yourself as a leader.

1. Involve your family

Your family is an incredible ministry resource. If you can't motivate them, how can you expect to motivate anyone else? The Millennials are in desperate need of a ministry team. The greatest gift you can give to the Millennials is an example of a healthy family.

> **The greatest gift you can give to the Millennials is an example of a healthy family.**

Don't expect your spouse to fit into some stereotype of a youth pastor's spouse; that can be destructive. Your spouse is gifted by God and has a call to serve. You have a God-given responsibility to help your spouse discover those gifts and use them. I do everything I can to create an environment for my wife to be involved. For example, the first five years of our kids' lives I found all the babysitters. This allowed Jana to be involved with inactive ministry without worrying about them. I have also involved my parents, in-laws, and even my two little girls. My family adds value to every part of my life and ministry.

2. Involve the senior citizens

Leaders understand that students need the influence and wisdom of older people. There is no doubt that they bring a unique spiritual depth and credibility. Senior citizens have prayed for me, encouraged me, and supported me like no other group. I see them as leaders.

Every year, I would go and speak at the senior citizens' luncheon and say, "This is my annual meeting with my leadership team. The youth ministry is only great because of your support. This generation is being changed because you know how to pray." Then I would give each of them two names to pray for throughout the year and send birthday cards to.

One of the greatest leaders I had was Sam Jacobsen. Sam was a senior citizen with more energy than most youth pastors. He drove the bus everywhere, which allowed me the freedom to build relationships with the students. Whenever I would see Sam in the hallway I would stop and ask, "How are you doing?"

Sam's reply was consistent, "I am more than a conqueror through Christ who strengthens me." Sam's life taught our students about the strength of Christ. Don't tell me that senior citizens can't be involved. Sam will have something to say about that.

3. Involve young couples

Just because they are newly married does not mean that they don't have time to give. Newlyweds will follow a leader. Tom and Sydney Metcalf were two of my greatest leaders. Tom was a businessman, and Sydney taught in public school. They gave their energy and time to youth ministry. Tom still uses the principles he learned in our leadership meetings. He commented that those meetings trained him better than his job. Tom and Sydney are examples of a young couple that has made a tremendous impact in the lives of students.

4. Involve parents

The parents of your students are a great resource. Remember to be sensitive to their youth in your ministry. Be sensitive, but still involve the parents.

> **You limit your leadership team if you don't involve parents.**

Dale and Joyce McMillan had three students involved with my youth ministry. Both of them worked busy jobs. Their main ministry was to come on the winter retreat once a year and lead a team of cooks. They loved it, and they saved the youth ministry thousands of dollars by finding great deals. You limit your leadership team if you don't involve parents. Just ask the students who were impacted by Dale and Joyce McMillan.

5. Involve single adults

Students need godly examples of people living a single life. And single adults have the extra time to invest in students.

I remember when Kemi Holley indicated an interest in youth ministry. She was a 35-year-old, single, full of energy, and ready to impact students. She added a lot of maturity to our team. When I became the District Youth Director and needed an administrative assistant, Kemi was doing such a great job organizing events in the youth ministry that I asked her to fill the position. When people tell me that single adults are flaky, I tell them they have never met Kemi Holley.

6. Involve college-age adults

You need the energy, example, and influence of responsible college-age adults. Avoid those who are just trying to escape the reality of becoming adults.

I have heard complaints that college students are unreliable. That's an excuse used by people who don't know how to work with them. College adults make great leaders because, in many cases, they have been raised in your youth ministry. They know your philosophy. If you have done a good job of growing students, you will be amazed at how many of them will want to be on your leadership team after they graduate from high school.

One of the strongest college students I had was Stacy Newell. Stacy was involved with a drama ministry team at Northwest College and was very busy with work and other ministries. However, Stacy got involved. Yes, I had to be flexible, but it was worth it—just ask the students who Stacy impacted forever. She made a real difference.

7. Involve new people

Stand in the lobby and meet new people. They often want to be involved with a ministry. Don't assume that new people need to get to know the church and check it out for a while. The very thing that a new person needs might be a ministry opportunity. New people add a fresh perspective to your church and youth ministry.

8. Involve students

Students provide energy and fresh ideas. If you can't motivate students to be involved with youth ministry, you will never be able to involve adults. Students can preach, lead in worship, and be involved with almost every part of your youth ministry. The list is only limited by your imagination. However, don't involve students in the adult leadership team. Create a leadership team that is designed to involve them in ministry.

9. Involve church influencers

There are adults who influence the life and decisions of your church. Leaders identify these influential people and involve them. Go out of your way to involve board members, elders, deacons, and trustees. Involve adults who have been at your church for years. They know the history and can give you wisdom on the potential problems your new ideas may create. If you include the church influencers on your team, your youth ministry will have influence in the church. Some may call this a political move, but I call it smart. I sincerely want the advice, wisdom, and input of these influencers.

10. Involve any and all adults in your church

Once again, *every* adult in your church is a potential leader. Don't rule them out because they don't fit into some model. Perhaps one of the greatest leaders I had was my secretary at Renton Assembly, Karen Snowden-Jones. Karen had the kind of skills to work in any professional office and make top dollar, but she made a choice to be a part of my leadership team. I had a great ministry because of Karen.

---

12 Leadership Qualities of the Twenty-First Century Youth Pastor

Leaders chase after mentors.

Leaders grow daily.

Leaders have a clear vision.

Leaders take responsibility.

Leaders have a winning attitude.

Leaders reinvent themselves.

Leaders understand what they must do.

Leaders involve everyone.

Chapter 10

Appoint Them as Leaders

Appoint them as officials over thousands, hundreds, fifties, and tens. (Exodus 18:21)

He chose capable men from all Israel and made them leaders of the people, officials over thousands, hundreds, fifties and tens. (Exodus 18:25)

L eaders build a team.

Jethro understood that the only way for Moses to effectively touch all the people was to organize them into small groups and appoint leaders. Jethro said, "Moses, divide your people up into groups of thousands, hundreds, fifties, and tens. Appoint leaders over these particular groups of people."

The first step to building a leadership team is to select capable people. Then you need to appoint them as leaders. Discover all the potential adults you want, but if you don't have a place for them, what good does it do? You must create a structure and put systems in place that allow everyone to be involved everywhere, every time.

You cannot be an effective leader without being organized. You must have the ability to create a leadership model that people can understand, easily fit into, and find their place of ministry. The moment you ask someone to be involved with youth ministry, they will want to know, "What does that mean? What are my responsibilities? What is required?" If you can't answer these questions, you will never have a healthy team.

Strong and competent leaders will not sit and watch you preach. The kid youth pastor says, "Come and prove yourself. Then, after six months I may involve you in youth ministry." The leader says, "Here is where you fit in. Let's begin using your gifts from God. If you don't fit in here, we will create a structure just for you."

Develop an Adult Leadership Team

Create a leadership model that will involve the following type of leaders.

- *Leaders of tens*. These are leaders who pastor small groups of students.
- *Leaders of fifties*. These are leaders who can effectively lead specific ministries.
- *Leaders of hundreds*. This better be you if you want to develop a youth ministry over 100 students.
- *Leaders of thousands*. These leaders are rare. Few people are willing to pay the price to lead at this level.
- *Behind-the-scenes leaders*. These are the leaders who use their special gifts and abilities behind the scenes.

If you do this, you will be able to involve every adult in your church.

1. Develop directors—leaders of hundreds and fifties

Directors share the load of ministry every day by providing leadership to specific ministry areas. Develop directors to lead

- Junior-high ministries
- Senior-high ministries

- College-age ministries
- Campus ministry
- Small groups
- Outreaches
- Choir
- Drama

These leaders are the ones who provide leadership to the whole youth ministry. They give you their heart and soul. They know how you think, how you make decisions, and they help to develop the ministry vision. By understanding and believing in the big picture, they provide leadership to the whole team.

Your youth ministry will grow when you develop directors who take on the responsibilities and commitments of specific age groups and ministries. When your youth ministry grows, you will need to spend more time with the directors. At all times, be willing to train them one-on-one in how you think, why you make decisions, and how to improve their leadership skills.

2. Develop interns—leaders of fifties and tens

Interns are the leaders being trained for full-time ministry. Depending on their skill level, desires, and individual growth, interns can be involved in different ways. In my case, they had to be in pursuit of a college degree, which meant they were able to commit 10 to 15 hours a week.

Be willing to provide growth opportunities for them and involve them in your leadership meetings. Interns deserve your best. Pour time and energy into them. Treat them with respect. Interns will work their guts out for you, but don't treat them like slaves. Yes, your interns need to learn to be servants and they need to prove themselves, but don't belittle them and use them in ways that are inhumane. If you aren't ready to train and send out

Interns deserve your best.

Appoint Them as Leaders

young adults into full-time ministry, don't waste an intern's energy by abusing their "free" time and labor.

My internship ministry was called MIT (Ministers in Training). The greatest joy of my ministry life is seeing couples in full-time ministry today because of my investment in their lives.

3. Develop a youth staff—leaders of tens

The main focus of the youth staff is to provide leadership to the tens. Train them how to pastor a small group of students. Develop a leadership meeting that provides growth opportunities and tools. Don't keep the youth staff so busy that they can't put time and energy into loving and growing students.

Your priority and energy should be in building a youth staff that can effectively grow students. This is new thinking for many youth pastors. In order to grow your youth ministry, you have to change your focus from "student development" to "developing leaders." Your ministry will only grow as big as your ability to grow your youth staff—period. I can tell you the size of your youth ministry just by asking two questions.

- "How many trained adult leaders do you have?"
- "Have you effectively broken your students down into groups of tens?"

Your youth staff is involved with the ministry on a weekly basis. Their time commitment needs to be flexible. However, these leaders must commit to being regularly involved with the life of the youth ministry and connecting one-on-one with students.

4. Develop a support team—leaders behind the scenes

Support teams can give from one hour a day to one hour a year to your youth ministry. They are the adults who want to help out but don't have a lot of time or just want to be involved with behind-the-scenes ministry. There may be an adult in your church right now who only wants to help in his or her own area of expertise but can't show up every week. You may have an adult who wants to count your offering every Wednesday, or an adult who wants to drive the bus once a month. These adults could be your most valuable team members. This team gives you the ability to involve people who can truly share the load, free your youth staff to grow students, and who can provide maturity and wisdom to your youth ministry. This is the platform to ensure that any adult, regardless of the amount of time he or she may have, can be involved.

You can't live without a support team. If you don't have a support team, your youth staff will get overwhelmed with details—cooking food, cleaning buses, and taking role in class. There are adults in your church who would love to come and do these things.

Support teams are involved on an as-needed basis. I had a support team that came every week to our service, and a support team that helped once a year. I couldn't have done youth ministry without them.

Your support team doesn't need much training from you, but they need a lot of appreciation and a hug. They need personal encouragement. Give people a raise by praise. You will be amazed what a simple thank-you can do for a leader.

Develop Partnerships

Develop partnerships with ministries, organizations, and individuals who can provide a networking system. Partnerships make you stronger. Leaders understand that they can't do everything. There are ministries, organizations, and people all around who you need to connect with if you want to be a great youth pastor.

You need seven to ten partnerships in your youth ministry that increase your effectiveness as a leader. Find people and organizations that have strengths and resources you don't have.

Adult Leaders	Time	Training	How Many	Who	Value	Responsibilities
Directors "leaders over hundreds and fifties . . ."	Daily	Daily one-on-one	3–5 people	Secretary, spouse, department head, junior-high or senior-high directors, etc.	High	Everything
Interns "leaders over fifties and tens . . ."	Daily	Weekly	1–12 in most cases	Ministers in training, Master's Commission, department heads, etc.	High	Everything—but they are leaders, not slaves
Youth Staff "leaders over tens . . ."	Weekly	Twice a month	As many as possible	Any responsible adult	High	Leading small groups, new people, teaching, loving and pastoring students, etc.
Support Team	Monthly to annually	Encouragement	As many as possible	Parents, senior citizens, new believers, new people, singles, young adults, etc.	High	Driving bus, cleaning, setting up chairs, cooking meals, chaperoning, praying for one student, sending birthday cards, etc.

1. Partner with your senior pastor

Your senior pastor can help you succeed. He may not be the best at building a relationship with you, communicating with you, or even the best leader on the planet, but it is *your* job to involve him in your youth ministry. The best way depends on his gifts and desires. Involve him in such a way that it is a joy, not a burden. In my case, with Pastor Rick, I engaged him in ministry questions all the time. We would sit down and I would find out how to become a stronger leader with questions like, "How can I lead my leadership meetings better? . . . How can I preach better?" A healthy youth ministry complements the life and ministry of the church. You complement your church by partnering with your pastor, not competing with him.

2. Partner with strategic ministries

Strategic ministries can help you build a great youth ministry by

- Reaching campuses
- Growing students
- Providing worship songs
- Providing resources
- Planning mission trips

Find other ministries that specialize in particular areas, and build a relationship. Use them as a resource, and view them as a part of the leadership team.

3. Partner with your denomination

Currently, I serve as the Youth Ministries Leadership Coach for the Assemblies of God, but I am not writing as a district official. I am a leader who believes in partnership. If you are part of a fellowship that provides a platform for partnering together, do it. More can be done as a team

Appoint Them as Leaders

than as an individual. Get over the attitude that you don't need your denomination. That attitude will limit your youth ministry.

See your denomination as a ministry partner. Use them as a resource and a networking tool. This does not mean that you have to do every program and attend every meeting they offer, but you are limiting yourself if you don't partner together.

> ## See your denomination as a ministry partner.

4. Partner with other churches

Leaders understand that fine doctrinal differences or style preferences shouldn't hinder a relationship with other churches. Unite with the other churches in your community and focus together on the dream of reaching local school campuses. We need to set aside the issues that divide us and focus on the principles that unite us.

5. Partner with other youth ministries

Other youth ministries can bring out the best in you, even if they aren't in your area or part of your church's affiliation. Find ministries that are doing a better job and can challenge and encourage you. Leaders understand the need to discuss their ministry with other pastors.

I remember the day I received a call from Bret Allen in Concord, California. He wanted to get information about Friday Nite Hangout. We were able to share resources, ideas, and dreams. I sent him everything I had about Friday Nite Hangout. He sent me ideas about how to do illustrated messages. I flew to California just to see his youth services in action. He flew to Seattle to see me do a Friday Nite Hangout. We both ended up better youth pastors because of our relationship.

If you don't have two or three youth ministries that you are gleaning from, you are limiting your potential as a leader.

6. Partner with experts and specialists

Look for people who are experts in what they do and ask, "How can I involve them?" You have people in your church who are experts in carpentry work, landscaping, Web site design, graphic arts, and video editing. Involve them, and they will add an incredible strength to your ministry.

7. Partner with businesses

Build a relationship with local businesses that will strengthen your ministry. For example, I built a relationship with the local printing company. The consistency and excellence of our publications improved. We also partnered with local restaurants to get pizza for our new people, and we partnered with other companies that helped with our Friday Nite Hangout.

8. Partner with speakers

Find speakers who can build your youth ministry. Include them strategically. In ten years of youth ministry, I only invited a handful of speakers. However, the speakers I invited came often. They became a part of my leadership team, and the students loved them. In a very real sense, the speakers invested into the students because they were able to develop a relationship.

9. Partner with church staff and elders

The church staff and elders offer insights and gifts that will help you. Involve them by first asking them questions in their areas of expertise. If you have a counseling pastor, bring out his expertise in counseling students. The music pastor may have great insights for your choir or worship band. The children's pastor may enjoy speaking to the youth. Associates may love the opportunity to organize an outreach.

But don't expect them to partner with you if you don't partner with them. Go out of your way to be involved in their ministries too.

I can still remember Mark Kruger's support and encouragement. Mark is an elder at Renton Assembly. His ministry is in the area of encouragement. Mark wasn't on any particular leadership list, but he was a strategic part of my leadership team. Mark would go out of his way just to encourage Jana and me. His support and insight helped to make our youth ministry great.

> **The local campuses are not your enemies.**

10. Partner with local campuses

The local campuses are not your enemies. When I first started youth ministry, campuses were my opponents. The day I changed that view was the day God opened the doors to impact those campuses.

Develop a Student Leadership Team

Your student leaders are those who are actively involved in making the youth ministry happen. Your student leaders will add energy and insight to your youth ministry. They are the ones who will come early and leave late.

Train and grow your student leaders. Develop a leadership meeting with them on a monthly basis. At this meeting, equip, encourage, and empower them as leaders. Don't allow your student leaders to attend your adult leadership team meetings. Create a special training meeting just for them, and provide your student leaders with growth tools and opportunities.

Don't limit the amount of student leaders who want to be involved. Involve any students who are hungry to grow and learn. I recommend that you wait for students to be in high school to join the student leadership team.

Your student leaders lead campus ministry and are actively involved with your youth ministry.

Principles of Team Building

1. Be organized and flexible

Leaders are very organized and flexible at the same time. If a leader meets a person that doesn't quite fit into their particular mold, they find a way to involve them. I created my leadership model by meeting adults who wanted to be involved but didn't fit into my thinking. I adapted and so did they.

Be flexible. Just because a leader is on the support staff, don't say no if he or she asks to lead a small group. Let the person lead one or assist someone else in leading. If a leader on your youth staff is gifted in hospitality, that is what the leader should do. Flexibility means you are able to put their agendas above your leadership model at the appropriate times.

2. Discover people's gifts

Leaders put people first. If their gift is leading the tens and God did not call them to lead the fifties, fine. Don't belittle those gifts. If their gift is baking cookies and not leading a small group, encourage them. Leaders stretch people and also understand specific gifts and abilities. Coach people, but don't clone them. Stretch people, but don't

Appoint Them as Leaders

break them. People are miserable when they have to do something they were not called to do.

> **People are miserable when they have to do something they were not called to do.**

3. Don't get too excited about titles

There are many ways to refer to your leadership team. But when it is all said and done, titles don't impress anybody. Treat everybody as a first-class leader. Create a leadership model that works and functions as a team. Refuse to put any type of value on people because of their title or position. This is sick and will kill your team environment.

4. Avoid a hierarchy

Every team member is valuable. Hierarchies destroy teams. The goal is not to get someone to go from being on the support team to the youth staff. If the transition happens naturally, that's great. Someone may be on the youth staff and decide that being on the support team is more productive for their gifts.

Your first and only goal is to provide a leadership model that empowers people. A youth ministry is effective only when everybody is working together.

5. Print out your leaders' names

Printing a list of names keeps people accountable to the youth ministry, provides contact information for easier communication, and creates a visual that shows how many people are involved. All of that builds confidence throughout the church that trained adults are working with students. Plus, it builds momentum to involve other adults and becomes a prayer tool.

The following is an actual list of the leaders at Renton Assembly in November 1997. I gave this document to everybody I could.

Directors

Pastor Troy Jones	Youth Pastor
Mark Newell	Asst. Youth Pastor/Junior High Director
David Grieve	Senior High Director
Scott Lendzion	Wednesday Night Director
Jana Jones	Choir Director
Shami Grieve	Human Video Director

Youth Staff

Mark Ash
Michelle Bang
Tim Boness
Josh Crandall
Christy Eden
Tiesha Fields
Elizabeth Fisher
Jason Ford
Kelly Giesen
Jake Goetze
Dave Gustafson
Jeff Hoffman

Kemi Holley
Brittany Hulten
Khara Khrause
Salinda Littrell
Randy McMillan
Anna McMillan
Tim McConnell
Sydney Metcalf
Tom Metcalf
Seve Nelson
Stacy Newell
Jemi Overby

Toby Rodriguez
Therisa Ropp
Micah Ryan
Matthew Sanford
Nick Schmal
John Schorb
Melinda Seth
Allan Shaeffler
Kim Springer
Loveta Veristian
Thys Wallwork

Support Team

Bob Austin
Diane Austin
John Beck
Patty Beck
Carla Barrans
Jennie Cady
Ralph Cady
Mickie Dickenson
Bill Dolleman
Doreen Dolleman
Eddie Duarte
Sandy Duarte
Harry Duffield
Bert Fields
Linda Fields

Evan Hamilton
Nola Hassel
Warren Hassel
Don Hoffman
Sue Hoffman
Dan Hopper
Sam Jacobsen
Sandy Keidel
Terry Keidel
Mark Kruger
Larry Lichty
Loran Lichty
Sonny Lichty
Ken Littlefield
Julie McIntire

Dale McMillan
Joyce McMillan
Keith Morris
Jean Morris
Alvina Newell
Ivan Newell
Bess Owens
Alan Shannon
Karen Snowden-Jones
Sonny Sternod
Rosie Sunde
David Train
Larry Walker
Robb Wolfe
Sue Wolfe

Appoint Them as Leaders

12 Leadership Qualities of the
Twenty-First Century Youth Pastor

Leaders chase after mentors.

Leaders grow daily.

Leaders have a clear vision.

Leaders take responsibility.

Leaders have a winning attitude.

Leaders reinvent themselves.

Leaders understand what they must do.

Leaders involve everyone.

Leaders build a team.

Chapter 11

Have Them Serve

Have them serve as judges for the people at all times, but have them bring every difficult case to you; the simple cases they can decide themselves. That will make your load lighter, because they will share it with you. (Exodus 18:22)

They served as judges for the people at all times. The difficult cases they brought to Moses, but the simple ones they decided themselves. (Exodus 18:26)

L eaders empower people.

The only way for Moses to reinvent himself was to have the people serve, make decisions, and do the work of ministry. Moses had to stop ministering to all the people, stop being a lone ranger, stop being the answer man, and start leading. Jethro told Moses he must go beyond just appointing leaders, he must release them. That day changed Moses because he let the people share the load of ministry.

Ask yourself these questions:

- "What responsibilities can I delegate?"
- "What am I doing right now that someone else can do better?"
- "What are my leaders doing right now that some other leader could be doing?"

If you only select people and put their names on a list, you will not have an effective team. The challenge is not finding people, but finding significant ministry avenues for them. Strong leaders want to do more than watch. If your leaders don't use their gifts for God, you will lose them.

> **If your leaders don't use their gifts for God, you will lose them.**

Stop doing ministry yourself if you want the people to do the ministry. Get out of the way. Leaders empower others to serve and focus on the simple cases.

Equip Your Team

Teach them the decrees and laws. (Exodus 18:20)

You have to train people to serve. Stop telling them what to do and begin *training* them how to do it. Instead of griping that your leaders don't sit with students, train them how to love students. Instead of complaining that your leaders don't lead small groups, train them how to lead small groups. You will discourage your leaders if you fail to equip your leaders. Training builds confidence and motivation among your team like nothing else. Without proper equipping and training you will frustrate your team.

Leadership – Equipping = Frustration

Here are four practical ways to equip your team.

1. Bimonthly leadership meeting

These leadership meetings should become the most important part of your month. Your threefold goal is to equip, empower, and encourage your team during these times. At the end of the chapter, I will discuss five guidelines for leadership meetings.

2. Annual leadership retreat

The leadership retreat is a time to build relationships, grow as leaders, and pray together. It's where you dialog on leadership principles and grow as a team. Some of the greatest moments of my life were the annual leadership retreats every fall. It is amazing what you can accomplish by just spending some time with each other. Relationships are built when you swim, eat, play board games, and enjoy life together. The memories last a lifetime.

During one of my first leadership retreats, a bunch of us were hungry late at night. So we started looking for a 24-hour restaurant. We saw a group of students hanging out in the parking lot of a grocery store and stopped to ask for directions. While talking to them, the subject of church came up. I shared my faith, and my leaders were able to see me minister outside of the context of the youth building. That night, I taught more than a lesson on leadership; I lived an example.

3. Train one-on-one

Your leaders need you to invest in them personally. Take time to watch your leaders lead. Go out of your way to see them in action. Spend time with your leaders one-on-one. Encourage them. Discuss issues that will help them grow. Never do ministry alone. Involve your leaders in ministry with you. Always have one of your leaders watching you lead. This kind of training will bring out the best in your leaders.

4. Provide growth opportunities

There are countless growth opportunities you can use to grow your leaders. Take your team to a leadership conference and experience the motivation and brainstorming that occurs when listening to others discuss youth ministry. Listen to a growth tape together. Read a book and discuss it. Visit a youth ministry and learn together. Your goal is to grow your leaders so much that they can pastor your students without you.

Empower Your Team

... that will make your load lighter, because they will share it with you. (Exodus 18:22)

An empowered leader is excited to be involved, has discovered their meaning in life, and works with passion and determination. He or she wants to make your load lighter by sharing the work with you. If you are not willing to share the load, your leadership team will get discouraged.

Leadership – Empowerment = Frustration

There are four things you must share with your leaders to empower them.

1. Share responsibility

Your leaders must understand the responsibility of reaching this generation for Christ. They are not your servants; they are fellow ministers. Every adult on your leadership team must take ownership to pass on the legacy to the next generation.

Help every leader see the importance of their ministry and how it fits into the overall strategy. When leading a small group, let them know they are having a significant impact on the future of those students.

The way they worship and respond will be cemented in the minds of those students for generations. Youth ministry is not a game; it is a responsibility. Help leaders understand that every time they set up a chair they are helping a student to hear the gospel. If they pick up garbage on the property, they are responsible for changing someone's image of the church.

2. Share authority

> Have them bring every difficult case to you; the simple cases they can decide themselves. (Exodus 18:22)

You cannot give someone responsibility without authority. If you make every decision, your youth ministry will never grow. Healthy leadership teams can make decisions without you. Jethro said, "Let them decide the simple cases." Relax and don't be so insecure. You don't have to be involved in every little decision that is made.

Before I make any big decision, I talk to my team. Most of the time we go to Starbucks to trade insights. Asking someone what he or she thinks motivates him or her more than you can imagine. You will be amazed at how your leaders become empowered when you share the decision-making process.

It has been said that 80 percent of the decisions a leader makes could be made just as well by any high-school sophomore. It's the other 20 percent that they are getting paid for.

> **When something goes right, blame your leadership team.**

This is the *80/20 Rule*. Leaders concentrate on the critical 20 percent and let their team concentrate on the rest.

Plenty of people sitting in your church can decide the "simple cases" for you. Don't rob them of a blessing or hinder the growth of your ministry by making the decisions yourself. In many cases they can decide better than you.

3. Share glory

A good leadership rule: When something goes right, blame your leadership team. When something goes wrong, take responsibility. We can accomplish a lot for God if we stop trying to get the glory.

4. Share workload

Involve everybody you can. Instead of having your youth staff do everything, let them focus on the students. Your church has a lot of responsible people who would love to share your work.

Here is a list of common youth ministry tasks with some suggestions on who can do them. There is no right or wrong answer here.

- *Take attendance.* Parents or senior citizens can take the attendance. They love to do it, and their presence adds value to your ministry.
- *Clean the bus.* Students, parents, and adults enjoy this; don't automatically yell at your interns to slave away. Be a leader; find people to get involved.
- *Run an inflatable.* Many times the inflatable company brings someone to run it, but there are adults who would love to come out and donate their own time.
- *Teach a Sunday school class.* Directors and interns should be teaching Sunday school, but you may know other people who can speak on specialized subjects. Bring in those senior citizens and single adults. If you do, you will be amazed at who else can invest in your students.
- *Lead a small group.* It should be the goal of every member of the youth staff to pastor and provide leadership for students in a small group.
- *Set up chairs.* Anyone can do this, but there are people who would love to do it every Wednesday if they knew it was making a difference.

- *Build props.* If a contractor in your church can help out, why make your youth staff and interns do this? They should be loving students. However, if your youth staff likes building things, go for it.
- *Web site design.* Many students can do this for you, or you can partner with a company.
- *Soundman.* This is a great ministry for any responsible adult in your church.
- *Drive the bus.* Stop driving the bus. Find a senior citizen who has some extra time. You will be able to focus more on the students.
- *Refreshments.* There are moms who would love to provide refreshments for you. Then your spouse wouldn't have to run around at the last minute, trying to find something.

Encourage Your Team

It is amazing what a thank-you will do for someone involved with your ministry. Trust me on this: If you spend your life encouraging people, you will never lack leaders. Lack of encouragement causes frustration. Make it your business to let people know that you appreciate them and couldn't do ministry without them.

Leadership – Encouragement = Frustration

When a leader says, "God is moving me to another ministry," that actually means: "Nobody has showed me any appreciation." If you

Praise your people.

don't take care of the leaders you have now, why would God give you more? Your leaders will eventually get frustrated and quit if they don't get encouragement from you.

Here are five ways to encourage your team.

1. *Praise your people*

Appreciate them; it's free. When appreciation is sincere and personal, people will die for you. In ministry, you have to build a team without the luxury of motivating people with money. Ministry is built on the backs of volunteers, and a simple thank-you often goes farther than a dollar bill.

2. Create a team environment

Become an expert on creating a team. On one of my leadership retreats, I began my teaching with the question, "What makes a great team?" After a few moments of their responses, I said, "Let's go see a great team in action." I then surprised my leaders with tickets to a Mariners game. We loaded up the bus and drove to the Kingdome. It was a great time building memories together and learning teamwork.

The next morning, I asked again, "What makes a great team?" We had a good discussion on what baseball and youth ministry have in common.

3. Believe in people

People can tell if you truly believe in them. When someone knows it, he or she will die for you. Never stop believing in people. I am often accused of believing in people too much. But if I am going to err, I am going to err on the side of seeing someone's possibilities, not his or her problems.

4. Invest in people

Investing in people goes way beyond finances; it takes real time and energy. If you are not getting a good return from your leaders, you may not be making the proper investments. Treat them with respect. Remember their birthdays, and spend time with them outside the ministry. Buy them a leadership book. Do whatever it takes to invest in them as people. These little things make a big difference.

5. Celebrate your wins

Everybody wants to be involved with a winning team. Learn how to celebrate, and look for reasons to shout. Give your leadership team the credit. Let them know that victory occurred because of their hard work. Celebrate when someone gets saved, when you have a successful event, or when one of your leaders does something new. Celebrate when another leader joins the team or when students sign up for discipleship.

Five Guidelines for Effective Leadership Meetings

Your leadership meetings should instill practical leadership principles that make your team better Christians, adults, workers, spouses—and leaders. The purpose of your leadership meeting is not to belittle your leaders or hype them up on a program. Your purpose is very simple:

> **If you don't plan, you don't deserve leaders.**

equip, empower, and encourage your leaders. After every meeting, answer these questions honestly,

1. "Did I *equip* my leaders with a skill that added value to their lives?"
2. "Did I *empower* my leaders during this meeting?"
3. "Did I *encourage* my team?"

An effective leadership meeting equips, empowers, and encourages your team. Here are five guidelines for an effective leadership meeting.

1. Keep them short

Keep leadership meetings under an hour. It doesn't have to be a marathon. Be honest! Do your leadership meetings go long because you haven't taken the time to prepare? If you don't plan, you don't deserve leaders.

When your leadership team grows to the point that you have directors responsible for specific ministries, you will want to give them an extra 30 minutes to meet with their own teams. This gives your directors a platform to lead and a time to discuss practical details that pertain to their specific ministries.

2. Arrive early

If you are late or show up right on time to the meeting, you send a loud message that you don't care. Your leadership meeting should be the most important thing that you do. Be early. Jana and I would arrive one hour early to our leadership meetings. The leaders knew that if they wanted to come early and just talk, we were there. They also knew that we valued their time so much that there was no way we would come running in at the last moment.

> ## Your leadership meeting should be the most important thing that you do.

3. Choose your best time

Don't compromise your leadership times. I once tried to conduct a leadership meeting right before our midweek church service. It was horrible. That's not when I am at my best, and that is also the time we should've all been hanging out with students. The best time for my leaders was Sunday at 4:00 P.M., before the evening service. This gave us plenty of time; Sunday nights weren't pressured for me. I was able to give them my best. You need to look at your calendar and reserve the best time of your week for your leaders.

4. Create a leadership environment

Don't run your meetings like a glorified Sunday school class. Treat your leaders like leaders. Think like a leader and cast vision. Create a conference atmosphere every time you meet. You need to train and motivate them better than they can find anywhere else. Like it or not, you create the spirit and attitude. If the attitude of your meetings is dry and mundane, it is because you are dry and mundane.

5. Develop a leadership agenda

The following step-by-step agenda is what I used for my leadership meetings.

a) *Pray* (5–7 min.). Prayer unites leaders together. My leadership meetings started at 4:00 P.M. sharp. If leaders walked in late, we were already standing and calling out to God. At the beginning, I would say something like, "What an incredible service we had last week. Five students gave their lives to Christ. Let's rejoice together and pray for them." Then we would lift up our voices and pray, whether holding hands or in small groups. Sometimes I would pray for a specific leader, sing a worship song, or pray for specific students.

b) *Grow and equip leaders* (25 min.). This was the most valuable time of the meeting. I would take a leadership lesson from one of the books I was reading and relate it to our youth ministry with questions, like

- "How do we grow as leaders?"
- "How do our attitudes impact us as leaders?"
- "How do we bring the best out of our students?"

Pick up any good book, such as John Maxwell's *21 Irrefutable Laws of Leadership*, and use it to teach 21 lessons. Have all of your leaders reading a leadership book or some youth ministry book together. Pick two or three books a year, and discuss the principles in detail. I trained my leaders to think, act, and live like responsible ministers. If you want your leaders to pastor your students, treat them like pastors. If you want your leaders to lead, teach them how.

c) *Leadership reception* (5–10 min.). This is when the leaders would just talk and encourage each other. Provide some light refreshments. This is your time to say thank-you to your leaders for all of their hard work. It's an important time but doesn't have to be fancy.

d) *Communication* (20–25 min.). This empowers your leaders with a regular time for communication and problem solving. I would communicate important information, cast vision, have brainstorming sessions, work on problems, and dream as a group. This is not a time to complain. Train your leaders to express their concerns privately with you.

e) *Directors' team meeting* (20–25 min.). Your meeting should be about one hour up to this point. Now your directors can have their own team meetings. Break them into junior high, senior high, college age, and other ministry groups. The directors of those particular ministries should lead the groups.

Survey Your Team Honestly

I recently had coffee with a youth pastor who was struggling with his leadership team and wanted a mentor. He loved God and his students, yet he was not a leader. Frustrated, he handed me a list of all his present youth leaders. Each name included a comment that he had personally written while taking a survey of his team. The problem was that he was making excuses and not being totally honest with himself. It was obvious why his leadership team was suffering. I read the piece of paper and gave him some very gut-level, honest advice.

Here is his list with my comments:

Tom: Had a personal problem with me from the beginning due to previous intern.

My response was, "You missed an opportunity to grow as a leader. You must learn to lead people who you don't like. Did you go out of your way to encourage this leader? Did you discuss the issues openly and honestly?"

Susan: Left with her daughter.

My response was, "My guess is that Susan used this as an excuse. The real reason was your lack of leadership. She was probably a stronger leader than you. Stronger leaders will always leave."

David and Lisa: Felt called to be involved in another ministry.

My response was, "This was just another way of saying, 'I don't like you.'"

Phil: Felt God was moving him on.

My response was, "He didn't want to hurt your feelings. God probably didn't tell him to move on. He moved because of you."

Elizabeth: Goes to another church.

My response was, "My guess is that Elizabeth was not happy with you. This was an excuse."

Tim and Connie: Involved only for a short time. Moved on to other ministries.

My response was, "I bet Tim and Connie didn't feel empowered and encouraged. When was the last time you said thank-you?"

Jim: Involved in an internship at another church.

My response was, "Why aren't you training interns?"

Joe and Kathy: Struggled in their personal lives. Gradually phased out.

My response was, "Did you ever train these leaders in their personal lives? Maybe they would still be there."

Diana: She is a mother of four and is very committed and involved as much as she can be.

My response was, "Who cares that she doesn't attend the youth staff meetings? Create a team that can use her gifts for God. Praise her for giving as much as she can. Don't belittle her for this."

Robert: 21 years old and single. Works at the church as the setup guy. Very involved and committed.

My response was, "Great, but is this where he is gifted?"

Nick: 22 years old and single. Works at the church as security. Is very involved and committed.
My response was, "Maybe he should be a director. Involve a leader like this to the fullest. Your youth ministry will explode if you get more directors involved in the ministries."

Sean and Shari: 18- and 21-year-old newlyweds. Minimal involvement.
My response was, "Have you asked them what kind of involvement they want? They may be the miracle you are looking for."

The youth pastor sat there with tears in his eyes. For the first time, he understood that he was blaming everybody else for his lack of leadership. He woke up and became a new leader. Being honest with yourself is the first step toward real change.

---

12 Leadership Qualities of the Twenty-First Century Youth Pastor

Leaders chase after mentors.

Leaders grow daily.

Leaders have a clear vision.

Leaders take responsibility.

Leaders have a winning attitude.

Leaders reinvent themselves.

Leaders understand what they must do.

Leaders involve everyone.

Leaders build a team.

Leaders empower people.

Chapter 12

Moses Listened

Moses listened to his father-in-law and did everything he said.
(Exodus 18:24)

L eaders listen.
One of the most insightful comments on the life of Moses is that he listened. Moses' Jethro Experience began with him talking and ended with him listening. A true Jethro Experience will shut you up. Moses had a choice: Listen to his father-in-law and change, or allow success and pride to stop him from growing.

Great leaders listen much more than they talk. At the beginning of the story, Moses talked. At the end of the story, Moses listened. Until you are ready to listen you will never be able to grow. Moses' whole ministry was saved because he listened to his father-in-law. Think about this: The entire nation of Israel was saved, a man's whole life was rearranged, and history was altered because one man, namely Moses, listened.

1. God

The only way you can effectively lead the Millennials is to be sensitive to the voice of God. We can't afford to ignore the small, still voice of God in our youth ministries. If you don't listen to God's voice, your ministry will never be effective. Often, God has given me clear direction or a warning in my spirit that helped me to avoid a lifetime of regret.

> **Whatever it takes, learn to hear the voice of God.**

We live in a fast-paced world. Discipline yourself to simply listen to the One who called you into the ministry. While driving, put down the cell phone and listen. Before you go to bed at night, ask God to speak to you. Instead of watching TV at night, take a walk and listen to him speak. Whatever it takes, learn to hear the voice of God.

If God is not speaking, you are not listening. If you are not listening to God, you are not the leader.

2. Mentors

Moses saved his ministry and the nation of Israel because he listened to Jethro. Before you make big decisions, get the wisdom of your mentors. But if you are not willing to listen, don't waste their time.

3. Intuition

Listen to your gut instinct. I have learned that my gut instinct is almost always right. You will be sorry every time you ignore it. Those are God's red flags and warning signs in your spirit. Learn to recognize them. If you don't, you will never have the God-given wisdom to lead this generation. Wisdom—not just another great idea—is what you need to lead your youth ministry. Wisdom will help you know when to listen and when to speak. Wisdom will let you know when to launch an idea or when to wait. Wisdom is a gift to a leader. Without wisdom you will destroy your youth ministry, church, and your own life.

People ask me,

- "How do you discern someone's gifts?"
- "How fast should you involve someone in ministry?"
- "When do you let someone teach or share with the students?"
- "How do you deal with problems?"
- "How do you move a person from one ministry to another?"
- "How do you deal with a leader who has an attitude problem?"

You must learn how to listen to your instinct. You can read all you want, but if you don't know how to listen to your instincts, reading becomes only a source of knowledge and not wisdom. Leaders develop great instincts and trust them.

4. Spouse

Your spouse is God's gift. So many men need to stop and listen to their wives. You may be living with the very person who can unlock growth in your youth ministry. When you learn to listen, your ministry will explode.

Jana and I never make a big decision unless we are in total unity. Sure, there are times when one of us will hesitate, but it is amazing how right Jana has been concerning people and circumstances. If I don't listen to her, I am being foolish. God has given your spouse as a defender. She sees things that you don't or can't. Together, you are one spirit and one flesh. Why ignore this God-given asset? Her input and insights are there to guarantee you continually succeed.

Most of the youth ministers who have fallen morally started their decline by refusing to listen to the warnings from their loving and concerned partners in ministry. Men, listen up!

5. Senior pastor

Your senior pastor is a God-given authority. Seek his advice and listen to it. Don't complain about your senior pastor not talking to you if you're not listening to him. Healthy communication begins with one person who is truly willing to listen. The day you start listening to your senior pastor is the day your relationship begins to change.

I made it my business to listen to Rick Ross.

- I listened while he preached so I could understand his heart.
- I listened at staff meetings so I could understand how to help him.
- I listened when he was frustrated so I could understand his hurts.
- I listened when he was excited so I could understand his hopes.

Some youth pastors envy my relationship with Rick. It's a blessing. But make no mistake: Rick Ross only mentors listeners. Your senior pastor knows if you are a listener. If he isn't talking to you, maybe you aren't listening.

6. Adults in the church

God will send adults who can give you great insight on your youth ministry. Get rid of your attitude that adults are irrelevant to this generation and can't give you insights on leadership. That adult that you don't particularly like may have the most important advice you need to hear. Don't allow your pride and defensive spirit to stop you from listening. Don't allow yesterday's successes to hinder you from achieving more successes in the future.

If someone has been alive longer than you, they probably have a better perspective than you. Listen! Yes, they will be wrong at times. Yes, they don't always say it with the right attitude. At the appropriate time, discuss the attitude behind the advice. Some of the greatest advice I have ever received came from adults who had wrong attitudes. Ignore the attitude and listen to the advice. Even if the advice isn't always right, your listening ear will create better teamwork among the members of the church.

7. Students

Leaders listen to the people they lead. Students can bring new insights on building a youth ministry. Listen very carefully to what your students are saying and what they are *not* saying. Don't assume that they are just being negative and unsupportive. Your students have new ideas and concepts that can grow your youth ministry. Your students are in tune with their peers and this generation. You will never be a great leader if you just think, *I am the leader; they are the sheep*.

If you want to be great in youth ministry, you must watch and study students. Recently, one of my students said to me, "Troy, the thing that keeps you effective with students is that you listen to us." You will only be effective with students if you care enough to ask about who they are and what they like to do.

8. Your critics

Your critics may save your ministry. Right or not, you can gain wisdom from their advice. Their real message is usually behind what's actually spoken. Leaders find the message that will help them grow.

Recently, I was at a restaurant, enjoying a cup of coffee with a youth pastor, when my cell phone rang. I answered the call, talked, and then got another call. A lady looked at me and then gave me a note as she left. I thought it would be something positive from someone who might have heard me speak. It wasn't. She tore into me, saying that I was rude because I had ignored my guest. She said I didn't care about people. I was furious—there was not an ounce of teachable spirit in me. I thought, *How dare this lady! She doesn't know me. I have never met her.* Then I stopped and realized she was right. I hadn't been respecting the person I was with, and I had been insensitive to the other people in the restaurant.

I do care about people, but that day I learned how to be more hospitable to my guests. I have changed my cell phone habits and have learned a valuable lesson from a critic. That lady was used by God to help Troy Jones grow.

---

12 Leadership Qualities of the Twenty-First Century Youth Pastor

Leaders chase after mentors.

Leaders grow daily.

Leaders have a clear vision.

Leaders take responsibility.

Leaders have a winning attitude.

Leaders reinvent themselves.

Leaders understand what they must do.

Leaders involve everyone.

Leaders build a team.

Leaders empower people.

Leaders listen.

Chapter 13

If You
Do This

If you do this and God so commands, you will be able to stand the strain, and all these people will go home satisfied. (Exodus 18:23)

Moses . . . did everything he said. (Exodus 18:24)

He chose capable men from all Israel and made them leaders of the people, officials over thousands, hundreds, fifties, and tens. They served as judges for the people at all times. The difficult cases they brought to Moses, but the simple ones they decided themselves. (Exodus 18:25–26)

L eaders follow advice.

It is one thing to listen, but it's another thing to *do* something. If you avoid change, you will continue to have the same problems, situations, and results. A true Jethro Experience will change the way you live. You won't grow until you change. There's no credit for listening and no credit for reading a great youth ministry book. People will only give you credit after you actually change. Moses *did* everything Jethro said. Moses went beyond listening; he changed.

And God so Commands

One of my favorite lines in this whole story is "and God so commands." Think about Jethro's wisdom. He didn't try to force Moses into a corner or manipulate him by saying, "This is God's will for your life." He wanted Moses to think for himself. He actually gave Moses a way out by saying, "I will give you some advice." Jethro wanted Moses to discover how to become a healthy leader and make decisions with the right motivations. A good mentor doesn't tell you what to do; he gives you room to make your own decisions.

"If you do this," two things will happen in your life and ministry.

1. You will enjoy youth ministry

You will be able to stand the strain. (Exodus 18:23)

Youth ministry is a joy. There is no greater honor in this world than ministering to the Millennials. If you are burned out, reinvent yourself or get out of youth ministry. God wants you to look forward to the next youth service and to have an inner passion for students.

> **If you are burned out, reinvent yourself or get out of youth ministry.**

The only way you can enjoy youth ministry over the long haul is to become a leader and build a team around you. If you attempt the entire ministry by yourself, you will burn out. If you stagnate, you will die. But "If you do this," your youth ministry will be enjoyable once again.

I have been involved with youth ministry for 14 years. Why is youth ministry a joy for me? Why do I still like students? I have learned how to build teams. It isn't overcomplicated or too spiritual. It's simple: Build a team and you will stand the strain. If you don't build a team, the stress will destroy you.

There is something that happens when a leader reaches the age of 30. They get tired of all-night parties, sleeping at retreat centers, and cleaning the bus. Just because you are tired of these things doesn't mean you are done with them. Don't get out of youth ministry; rethink how to build a team.

2. Your students will grow

... and all these people will go home satisfied. (Exodus 18:23)

Our responsibility is to grow students, not entertain them. The greatest legacy you can leave in the hearts of students is to influence them to become lifetime growers. The test of youth ministry is not what happens to the student while they are with you, but what happens when they leave.

The vision of youth ministry is to see students become adults who love Jesus. The vision is not to provide them with fun activities and baby-sit them until they graduate. When youth ministry is all said and done, the result should be changed lives—godly husbands, strong church elders, future ministers, loving mothers, and adults who take God's desires into the working world.

Because of my adult leadership team, there are students who are serving God today as adults. I don't know how many, but the thought of that legacy encourages me to keep training more adults who will impact more students.

Laura Krisel entered my youth ministry at the age of 13. She was a typical teenager. Without healthy adults in her life, she would have drifted away from God. If I did ministry alone, where would Laura Krisel be today? Because of the strong leaders who surrounded her, I don't have to answer that question. Laura has just completed a two-year internship with a missions organization and is planning on attending Northwest College in Kirkland, Washington. She is one of thousands of students who are serving God today because of the adults who cared enough to invest in their lives.

If You Do This

> If you do this and God so commands, you will be able to stand the strain, and all these people will go home satisfied. (Exodus 18:23)

Moses chose capable people from all over Israel and developed a leadership model that involved all types of leaders. Then he got out of their way and let them serve. Wow! Moses became one of the greatest leaders in the history of mankind. How? He had enough wisdom to follow the advice of someone who was smarter.

Today, everyone has access to information, but information by itself doesn't do you any good. The one who applies the information wins, not the one with the information. Moses did exactly what Jethro told him, and he didn't waste time. He didn't say, "Tomorrow, . . ." or, "In my next position I will . . ." or, "I'll pray about it." He immediately put into practice the advice of a good mentor.

Leaders put into practice the principles they learn. They don't waste time. Why should your mentor give you any more advice if you aren't following the last piece of advice? If the principle is not applied today, chances are good that the principle will never be applied. Anyone can listen. Few change. You are not teachable until you follow advice. This is the essence of leadership.

Start today. Don't waste time. Begin building a team!

This is the heart of this book: We must change if we want to grow. Moses went beyond the advice he received. He wasn't satisfied just to listen to a leadership tape and glean great insights without changing internally. Moses followed through. Some of us just keep going from conference to conference, book to book, and advice to advice. Stop reading and not changing. Stop getting advice without following through. Be proactive with what you have learned. If you do this, your church may not recognize their new youth pastor. If you don't do this, your church may fire their old youth pastor.

The choice is yours. I believe you can make it. There has never been a greater day for youth ministry than now. We have an opportunity to impact students and enjoy a God-given legacy.

---

12 Leadership Qualities of the Twenty-First Century Youth Pastor

Leaders chase after mentors.

Leaders grow daily.

Leaders have a clear vision.

Leaders take responsibility.

Leaders have a winning attitude.

Leaders reinvent themselves.

Leaders understand what they must do.

Leaders involve everyone.

Leaders build a team.

Leaders empower people.

Leaders listen.

Leaders follow advice.

Questions and Answers

The following are real questions that people have asked during leadership courses all over the nation.

Question: You have encouraged us to involve everybody in our youth ministry? Where do you draw the line?

Answer: My passion is to involve everyone, everywhere, every time. However, if an adult has been accused of any kind of child molestation, they are never allowed to be involved in my youth ministry. This is very difficult for me to say, but wisdom dictates that they can't be involved.

Question: Can we use unbelievers in our youth ministry?

Answer: You can't use unbelievers to pastor a group of ten students or to teach a Sunday school class. However, you can use unbelievers to work behind the scenes. An unbeliever built our first laser-tag arena. It was a great chance to minister to him. I didn't put him on a particular list, but he was a great help.

Question: What if I don't trust someone on my leadership team?

Answer: Don't work with someone you don't trust. First, do everything you can to build the trust factor into the relationship. Spend time with them, get to know their heart, and build a one-on-one rapport. If you can build trust, you can build a leader.

Question: What if I have people on my youth staff who should be on the support team?

Answer: It takes time to transition to a leadership model that includes directors, interns, youth staff, and a support team. Don't worry! The important thing is how they are using their gifts. People are more important than the structure. Eventually, those people will see the need to change what team they are on.

Question: What if there is a negative feeling over the youth ministry in my church?

Answer: There is only one way to change negative morale: Change it. It doesn't matter why the feeling exists. It may have been the leader before you. It may be some circumstance that you don't have control over. A good leader will eventually change a poor environment.

Question: How do I begin building my team?

Answer: Begin with Step 1: Select capable people. Open your eyes and see the leaders sitting in your church. Begin to see everyone as a potential leader in your youth ministry.

Question: How do you deal with leaders who have a problem with your wife?

Answer: The first question you should ask is, "Does your wife have a problem?" If your wife really needs to change, start there.

Question: My senior pastor won't mentor me, what do I do?

Answer: Read chapter 2.

Question: What if I have leaders who don't know when to share their opinions?

Answer: Train them. You need a leadership meeting that equips, empowers, and encourages leaders. Discuss how to have healthy disagreements. Share with them *how* to disagree before you disagree.

Question: How long should I know a person before I involve him or her?

Answer: The moment I meet a person I begin to examine his or her gifting. You can begin to involve a person immediately. Just be careful that you don't hand over a public ministry until you have had time to examine his or her personal character.

Question: What if people think one team is more important than another team?

Answer: First, make sure your attitude is right. Then, be sure you always refer to them as one adult leadership team. You are all on the same team, and everyone is valuable. Everyone working together makes the youth ministry great.

Question: Can I involve a wife and not a husband?

Answer: Absolutely.

Question: How many leaders do I need?

Answer: You need as many leaders as possible—the more, the better.

Bibliography

Barna, George. *Third Millennium*. The Barna Research Group, Ltd., 1999.

Begley, Sharon. "A World of Their Own." *Newsweek*, May 8, 2000, p. 54–56.

Cohen, Jodi S. "'Echo Boomers' Hip and High-tech Savvy." *Detroit News*, November 29, 1998. http://detnews.com/1998/metro/9811/29/11290089.htm.

Elkind, David. *All Grown Up and No Place to Go*. Cambridge: Perseus Books, 1998.

Featherstone, Vaughn, J. *The Millennial Generation*. Desert Book Company, 1999.

Hutchcraft, Ron. *The Battle for a Generation*. Chicago: Moody Press, 1996.

Johnson, Steven. *Interface Culture*. New York: Basic Books, 1997.

Joyal, Vicki. "Meet the Millennials." *News Now*. April 23, 2000.

Long, Jimmy. *Generating Hope*. Downers Grove: Intervarsity Press, 1997.

McAllister, Dawson. *Saving the Millennial Generation*. Nashville: Thomas Nelson Publishers, 1999.

McDowell, Josh and Hostetler, Bob. *Right from Wrong*. Nashville: Word Publishing, 1998.

Naisbitt, Nana and Philips, Doug. *High Tech High Touch*. New York: Broadway Books, 1999.

Nash, Robert N., Jr. *An 8-track Church in a CD World.* Macon: Smyth & Helwys, 1997.

Quindlen, Anna. "Now It's Time for Generation Next." *Newsweek,* January 1, 2000.

Rainier, Thom S. *The Bridger Generation.* Nashville: Broadman & Holman Publishers, 1997.

Strauss, William and Howe, Neil. "The Battle for the Millennial Generation." Nov. 24, 1997. http://www.fourthturning.com; April 23, 2000.

Sweet, Leonard. *Soul Tsunami: Sink or Swim in New Millennium Culture.* Grand Rapids: Zondervan, 1999.

Tapscott, Don. *Growing Up Digital.* New York: McGraw-Hill, 1998.

Tasker, Fred. "Here Come the Millennials" *The Seattle Times,* July 31, 1997. http://archives.seattletimes.com/cgi-bin/texis/web/vortex/display?slug=mill&date=19970731.

Woodyard, Chris. "Generation Y—The Young and the Boundless Are Taking Over Pop Culture." *News.* October 6, 1998.

PRODUCT DESCRIPTION

If You Do This, Your Church May Not Recognize Their New Youth Pastor, by Troy Jones - $11.99

Discover the leadership role of today's youth pastor. In *If You Do This, Your Church May Not Recognize Their New Youth Pastor*, Troy reveals the wisdom that Moses received from his father-in-law Jethro in Exodus 18. Learn practical insights on how to build key leadership teams, maintain longevity, and empower spiritual gifts.

From Survival to Significance, by Troy Jones - $11.99

Are you ready to lead an effective youth ministry and grow students? Want to improve that important relationship with your senior pastor? This youth pastor survival guide will help you find the right way to establish lasting significance in your youth ministry.

Anoint Us worship CD - $14.99

Your spirit will come alive with God's heart for this generation as you hear over 5000 students praising God. Led by Jana Jones and a 300-voice youth choir, this inspiring collection of worship music was recorded live at the Northwest Youth Convention.

Power2Grow Devotional Software - $10.00

Develop a Bible reading plan that starts today and lasts a lifetime. This interactive software let's you print over 400 scriptures easily-great for memorization. Plus, you can develop a custom prayer list that fits conveniently in your Bible, purse, or desktop organizer. (Minimum system requirements: Windows 95/98, 32 MB RAM, CD-ROM drive, 600x800 screen resolution.)

Power2Grow Leader's Manual - $25.00

Change lives! Here's how to begin a Power2Grow discipleship ministry in your church. This leadership manual clearly outlines the ministry vision and takes you from start to finish through every important step.

Power2Grow Leadership Tape Series for Adult Leaders, by Troy Jones and Loran Lichty - $10.00

This two-tape series includes a closer look at Troy's life, attitudes, and leadership vision. Loran's teaching is some of the best in the nation for adult leaders who want to understand their leadership role in youth ministry.

Three Ways To Order Your Resources: 1) By Mail (see the attached order form), 2) online at www.power2grow.com 3) Email at sales@power2grow.com

Leadership Training Available

Power2Grow Ministries is committed to helping leaders and churches discover practical ways to grow. We provide training on leadership, youth ministry, finances and the family. These leadership training sessions are facilitated by Troy Jones and a number of other speakers across the nation.

The following are a few leadership training sessions that Power2Grow Ministries provides:

The Youth Pastor as Leader: This leadership training covers the five skills of the 21st century youth pastor.

Youth Ministry Health: This leadership training covers seven characteristics of a healthy youth ministry and helps youth pastors evaluate their area of strengths and weakness in their ministries.

Skin Against Skin: Troy and Jana discuss practical ways on how to have a healthy marriage and ministry at the same time.

The Youth Pastor as CEO: This leadership training takes a look at how youth pastors need to think, act and make decisions as a CEO.

Discovering Your Destiny: This leadership training helps Christians and leaders to discover their God given S.H.A.P.E and destiny in the Body of Christ and world.

Financial Freedom: This leadership training discusses principles of financial stewardship and freedom.

Schedule a Leadership Training with Power2Grow Ministries today by emailing us at customerservice@power2grow.com.